Idaho Legal Research

Carolina Academic Press
Legal Research Series

Tenielle Fordyce-Ruff, Series Editor
Suzanne E. Rowe, Series Editor Emerita

Arizona, Third Edition — Tamara S. Herrera
Arkansas, Second Edition — Coleen M. Barger, Cheryl L. Reinhart & Cathy L. Underwood
California, Fourth Edition — Aimee Dudovitz, Sarah Laubach & Suzanne E. Rowe
Colorado, Second Edition — Robert Michael Linz
Connecticut — Jessica G. Hynes
Federal, Second Edition — Mary Garvey Algero, Spencer L. Simons, Suzanne E. Rowe, Scott Childs & Sarah E. Ricks
Florida, Fourth Edition — Barbara J. Busharis, Jennifer LaVia & Suzanne E. Rowe
Georgia — Nancy P. Johnson, Elizabeth G. Adelman & Nancy J. Adams
Idaho, Third Edition — Tenielle Fordyce-Ruff
Illinois, Second Edition — Mark E. Wojcik
Iowa, Second Edition — John D. Edwards, Karen L. Wallace & Melissa H. Weresh
Kansas — Joseph A. Custer & Christopher L. Steadham
Kentucky, Second Edition — William A. Hilyerd, Kurt X. Metzmeier & David J. Ensign
Louisiana, Third Edition — Mary Garvey Algero
Massachusetts, Second Edition — E. Joan Blum & Shaun B. Spencer
Michigan, Third Edition — Cristina D. Lockwood & Pamela Lysaght
Minnesota — Suzanne Thorpe
Mississippi — Kristy L. Gilliland
Missouri, Third Edition — Wanda M. Temm & Julie M. Cheslik
New York, Third Edition — Elizabeth G. Adelman, Theodora Belniak, Courtney L. Selby & Brian Detweiler
North Carolina, Third Edition — Brenda D. Gibson, Julie L. Kimbrough, Laura P. Graham & Nichelle J. Perry
North Dakota — Anne E. Mullins & Tammy R. Pettinato
Ohio, Second Edition — Sara Sampson, Katherine L. Hall & Carolyn Broering-Jacobs
Oklahoma — Darin K. Fox, Darla W. Jackson & Courtney L. Selby
Oregon, Fourth Edition, Revised Printing — Suzanne E. Rowe & Megan Austin
Pennsylvania, Second Edition — Barbara J. Busharis, Catherine M. Dunn, Bonny L. Tavares & Carla P. Wale
Tennessee, Second Edition — Scott Childs, Sibyl Marshall & Carol McCrehan Parker
Texas, Second Edition — Spencer L. Simons
Washington, Second Edition — Julie Heintz-Cho, Tom Cobb & Mary A. Hotchkiss
West Virginia, Second Edition — Hollee Schwartz Temple
Wisconsin — Patricia Cervenka & Leslie Behroozi
Wyoming, Second Edition — Debora A. Person & Tawnya K. Plumb

Idaho Legal Research

Third Edition

Tenielle Fordyce-Ruff

Tenielle Fordyce-Ruff, Series Editor
Suzanne E. Rowe, Series Editor Emerita

Carolina Academic Press
Durham, North Carolina

Copyright © 2019
Tenielle Fordyce-Ruff
All Rights Reserved.

Library of Congress Cataloging-in-Publication Data

Names: Fordyce-Ruff, Tenielle, author.
Title: Idaho legal research / by Tenielle Fordyce-Ruff.
Description: Third edition. | Durham, North Carolina : Carolina Academic Press, LLC, [2019] | Series: Legal research series | Includes bibliographical references and index.
Identifiers: LCCN 2019021498 | ISBN 9781531015596 (alk. paper)
Subjects: LCSH: Legal research--Idaho.
Classification: LCC KFI75 .F67 2019 | DDC 340.072/0796--dc23
LC record available at https://lccn.loc.gov/2019021498

e-ISBN 978-1-5310-1560-2

Carolina Academic Press
700 Kent Street
Durham, North Carolina 27701
Telephone (919) 489-7486
Fax (919) 493-5668
www.cap-press.com

Printed in the United States of America.

To Suzanne—my teacher, mentor, and friend.
TFR

Summary of Contents

List of Tables and Appendices	xvii
Series Note	xix
Foreword	xxi
Preface and Acknowledgments for the Third Edition	xxiii
Chapter 1 · The Research Process and Legal Analysis	3
Chapter 2 · Preparing to Research and Organization Research Results	11
Chapter 3 · Research Techniques	23
Chapter 4 · Secondary Sources and Practice Aids	35
Chapter 5 · Constitutions	53
Chapter 6 · Statutes	61
Chapter 7 · Bill Tracking and Legislative History	73
Chapter 8 · Rules of Court and Professional Ethics	93
Chapter 9 · Administrative Law	97
Chapter 10 · Court Systems and Judicial Opinions	111

Chapter 11 · Researching Judicial Opinions	123
Chapter 12 · Citators	133
Chapter 13 · Legal Citation	139
About the Author	155
Index	157

Contents

List of Tables and Appendices	xvii
Series Note	xix
Foreword	xxi
Preface and Acknowledgments for the Third Edition	xxiii
Chapter 1 · The Research Process and Legal Analysis	**3**
I. Introduction to Idaho Legal Research	3
II. The Intersection of Legal Research and Legal Analysis	4
III. Types of Legal Authority	4
IV. Overview of the Research Process	6
A. Getting Started	7
B. Research Secondary Authorities	7
C. Research Enacted Law	8
D. Research Case Law	8
E. Update the Law	8
F. End Research	9
V. Researching the Law — Organization of This Book	9
Chapter 2 · Preparing to Research and Organization Research Results	**11**
I. Preparing to Research	11
A. Gathering Facts and Determining Jurisdiction	11
B. Generating Research Terms	13
C. Planning a Research Strategy	14

1. Which Process?	15
2. Determine Which Provider to Search	16
3. Creating Effective Searches	17
4. Select Search Techniques	18
II. Keeping Track of Research Results	18
A. Research Notes	18
B. Analytical Notes	18
III. Organizing Research Results	20
IV. Outlining the Analysis	21

Chapter 3 · Research Techniques — 23

I. The Structure of Legal Information	23
II. Online Legal Research Sources	24
A. Government and University Websites	24
B. Other Commercial and Free Providers	25
III. Conducting Research Using Lexis, Westlaw, and Other Services	26
A. Find by Citation	27
B. Table of Contents Searching	27
C. Using Search Terms	28
1. Natural Language Searching	28
2. Terms-and-Connectors Searching	29
D. Topic Searching	32
IV. Conducting Research in Print	33

Chapter 4 · Secondary Sources and Practice Aids — 35

I. Introduction	35
II. Selecting the Most Relevant Secondary Sources	37
III. Researching in Print or Online	38
IV. Treatises, Practice Guides, and Other Books	39
A. Treatises	40
B. Idaho Practice Guides	40
C. Finding and Using Legal Books	41
V. Legal Encyclopedias	41

VI. Legal Periodicals	42
A. Law Reviews and Journals	42
B. Bar Journals	44
C. Locating Articles	44
VII. *American Law Reports*	45
VIII. Continuing Legal Education Publications	46
IX. Forms	46
X. Mini-Libraries and Loose-Leaf Services	48
A. Print Resources	48
B. Online Services	49
XI. Restatements	50
XII. Uniform Laws and Model Codes	51
XIII. Jury Instructions	52

Chapter 5 · Constitutions   53

I. The Idaho Constitution	53
A. Researching the Idaho Constitution	54
1. Locating Constitutional Provisions	54
2. Interpreting the Idaho Constitution	54
3. Researching Related Cases	56
4. Researching the Constitution's History	56
II. Locating and Researching the United States Constitution	59

Chapter 6 · Statutes   61

I. Idaho Statutory Research	61
A. Structure of Idaho Statutes	61
B. Researching the Idaho Code	62
C. Researching the Idaho Code Online	63
1. Find by Citation	63
2. Tables of Contents Searching	63
3. Researching with Search Terms	64
4. Index Searching	65
D. Researching Idaho Statutes in Print	65
1. Finding by Citation	65
2. Searching the Index for Research Terms	65

E. Reading Statutes	66
F. Using Annotations: Finding Cases That Interpret or Apply Statutes	67
II. Applying and Interpreting Idaho Statutes	69
III. Researching the Statutes of Other States	70
IV. Federal Statutes	71
Chapter 7 · Bill Tracking and Legislative History	**73**
I. The Legislative Process	73
II. Idaho Bill Tracking	75
A. Researching with a Bill Number	76
B. Learning about Other Pending Bills	76
III. Idaho Legislative History Research	76
A. Sources of Idaho Legislative History	77
B. Compiling Idaho Legislative History	77
1. Review the Source Note for the Statute	77
2. Review the Session Laws	82
3. Find the Bill	82
4. Find the Statement of Purpose and Fiscal Note for the Bill	83
5. Find the Procedural History of the Bill	83
6. Find the Committee Minutes	83
7. Check for Other Sources of Legislative History	84
C. Researching Older History	84
IV. Initiative and Referendum in Idaho	84
V. Attorney General Opinions	85
VI. Federal Legislative Research	87
A. Federal Bill Tracking	87
B. Federal Legislative History	87
1. Sources of Federal Legislative History	88
2. Compiled Legislative History	88
3. Print Sources for Federal Legislative History	88
4. Online Sources for Federal Legislative History	88
Appendix. Examples of Idaho Legislative History	89

Chapter 8 · Rules of Court and Professional Ethics	93
I. Court Rules	93
A. Idaho Court Rules	93
B. Reading Rules	94
C. Federal Court Rules	94
II. Ethical Rules	95
Chapter 9 · Administrative Law	97
I. Administrative Law and Governmental Agencies	97
II. Administrative Rules	98
III. Researching Idaho Administrative Law	100
A. The Enabling Act	100
B. *Idaho Administrative Code*	100
C. *Idaho Administrative Bulletin*	103
1. Updating an Idaho Rule	103
2. Other *Bulletin* Information	103
D. Guidance Documents	104
E. Agency Decisions	104
IV. Researching Federal Administrative Law	105
A. *Code of Federal Regulations*	105
B. *Federal Register*	107
C. Updating a Federal Regulation	108
D. Decisions of Federal Agencies	108
E. Judicial Opinions	109
Chapter 10 · Court Systems and Judicial Opinions	111
I. Court Systems	111
A. Idaho Courts	112
B. Federal Courts	113
C. Courts of Other States	114
II. Idaho Judicial Opinions	114
A. Reporters for Idaho Cases	114
B. West's Regional Reporters	115
C. Citing Idaho Cases	116

D. Parts of a Reported Case	117
E. Tables in Idaho Reports	120
F. Slip Opinions and Advance Sheets	120
G. Idaho Cases Online	121
III. Federal Cases	121
A. Sources for United States Supreme Court Cases	122
B. Sources for United States Courts of Appeals Cases	122
C. Sources for United States District Courts Cases	122

Chapter 11 · Researching Judicial Opinions — 123

I. Find by Citation	123
II. Using Search Terms	124
A. Natural Language Searching	124
B. Terms-and-Connectors Searching	125
III. Leveraging Topical Connectivity: Digests	125
IV. Reading and Analyzing Cases	126
A. Basic Civil Procedure	127
B. Analyzing the Substance of Cases	128
C. Strategies for Reading Cases	130

Chapter 12 · Citators — 133

I. Citator Fundamentals	134
A. Accessing and Reading the Citator List	134
B. Review Analytical Symbols	135
C. Select Citation List Needed and Filter Results	136
D. Read the Results	137
E. Alerts	138

Chapter 13 · Legal Citation — 139

I. Citation as Language	139
II. Purpose of Legal Citations	139
III. Principles of Legal Citation	140
A. Core Identification Principles	140
B. Minimum Content Principles	140

C. Compacting Principles	141
D. Formatting Principles	141
IV. Idaho Citation — General Practices	142
V. Other States' Citation Rules	142
VI. National Citation Manuals	142
A. Navigating the *ALWD Guide* and the *Bluebook*	143
1. Index	143
2. "Fast Formats" and "Quick Reference"	143
3. *Bluebook* "Bluepages"	143
4. *ALWD* Appendices and *Bluebook* Tables	144
B. Citing Idaho Material	144
C. Incorporating Citations into a Document	145
D. Case Citations	146
1. Full Citations to Cases	146
2. Short Citations to Cases	149
E. Federal Statutory Citations	150
F. Signals	151
G. Explanatory Parentheticals	151
H. Quotations	152
VII. Additional Citation Details	152
VIII. Citations Not Covered by a Manual	153
About the Author	155
Index	157

List of Tables and Appendices

Tables

Table 1-1. Examples of Authority in Idaho Research	5
Table 1-2. Overview of the Research Process	7
Table 2-1. Preliminary Research Questions	12
Table 2-2. Generating Research Terms	14
Table 2-3. Planning a Research Strategy	15
Table 2-4. Sample Analysis Chart	22
Table 3-1. Online Research Websites	25
Table 3-2. Formulating Effective Terms-and-Connectors Searches	29
Table 3-3. Boolean Expanders, Placeholders, and Connectors	30
Table 4-1. Websites for Idaho Research	39
Table 4-2. Sample Idaho Form	47
Table 4-3. Restatement Topics	50
Table 5-1. Articles of the Constitution of Idaho	55
Table 5-2. Collateral References	57
Table 5-3. Compiler's Notes for Article I, § 7	58
Table 6-1. Chapters in Title 32, Domestic Relations	62
Table 6-2. Outline for Idaho Statutory Research	63
Table 6-3. Using Search Terms on Westlaw and Lexis	64

Table 6-4. Example Idaho Statute	67
Table 6-5. Requirements for Recording a Marriage Settlement	68
Table 7-1. Bill Tracking Online	75
Table 7-2. Legislative History Documents	78
Table 7-3. Excerpt from Idaho Code with Source Notes	80
Table 7-4. Excerpt from Idaho Session Laws 2002	81
Table 7-5. Selected Sources for Federal Legislative History in Print	89
Table 8-1. Idaho Court Rules	94
Table 8-2. Topics of Idaho Rules of Professional Conduct	95
Table 9-1. Example of Idaho Administrative Rule Numbering	99
Table 9-2. Outline for Idaho Administrative Law Research	100
Table 9-3. Excerpt from an Idaho Rule IDAPA 02.02.04.050	102
Table 9-4. Example of a Federal Regulation	106
Table 10-1. Regional Reporters and States Included	116
Table 10-2. Reporters for Federal Court Cases	121
Table 11-1. Conducting Effective Natural Language Searches for Judicial Opinions	124
Table 12-1. Outline for Using Online Citators	135
Table 12-2. Analytical Symbols for Lexis and Westlaw	136
Table 13-1. Example Citations Under Idaho Conventions	142
Table 13-2. Example Citations in ALWD and Bluebook Format	144
Table 13-3. Examples of Citation Sentences and Citation Clauses	145

Appendices

Appendix 7-A. Excerpt of Minutes from Senate Committee	89
Appendix 7-B. Statement of Purpose	91
Appendix 7-C. Online Daily Data Tracking History	92

Series Note

The Legal Research Series published by Carolina Academic Press includes titles from many states around the country as well as a separate text on federal legal research. The goal of each book is to provide law students, practitioners, paralegals, college students, laypeople, and librarians with the essential elements of legal research in each jurisdiction. Unlike more bibliographic texts, the Legal Research Series books seek to explain concisely both the sources of legal research and the process for conducting legal research effectively.

Foreword

Chief Justice Roger S. Burdick,
Idaho Supreme Court

Without a clearly worded, thoroughly and honestly researched theory, followed by a logical analysis of facts to the theory, practitioners and students will not be successful in advocating their client's cause. *Idaho Legal Research* can help students acquire the skills they need to research legal theory and apply the law to their client's problems; it can also help Idaho practitioners refresh and update their research skills.

This book will give you a framework with which to go forward in the preparation of zealously advocating for your client. It not only provides a general framework that can be found in a number of general research guides, but most importantly for those of us practicing in Idaho, it is specific to our needs. This tailoring of general to specific is especially helpful in the use of our constitutional history, our specific quirks of procedure and pleading, and our use of authority. This book contains material, advice, and techniques that every attorney should consult over the course of her career. *Idaho Legal Research* integrates all methods of research and details the sources of law that are important to Idaho attorneys.

With the new edition, *Idaho Legal Research* has been updated to stay current with the constantly evolving research tools available through online sources. Any attorneys undertaking a research project in an unfamiliar area of the law would be well served by consulting this book as the first step in effective and efficient research. *Idaho Legal Research* is a fine book for students, as well as practitioners, now and in the future. This is truly a book for Idaho lawyers.

Preface and Acknowledgments for the Third Edition

This third edition of *Idaho Legal Research* continues the goal of prior editions: to explain clearly and concisely the sources and the process for researching Idaho law. This edition increasingly emphasizes online research and the strategies to help researchers use online services effectively, while including essential guidance with print sources that remain relevant. Most chapters have been substantially revised to embrace the shift to online case research. New chapters on preparing to research and research strategies have also been added.

I attempt to present a balanced coverage of Lexis and Westlaw, as they are the most widely used online research services. I also attempt to include guidance on lower-cost and free services and indicate when using a free or low-cost resource would be a better choice for researching.

I also want to express my deep gratitude and appreciation to Suzanne Rowe at the University of Oregon School of Law, my co-author on the first edition, and Kristina Running at the University of Idaho College of Law, my co-author on the second edition. While this edition includes substantial changes from the first two, their work is reflected throughout. Any of their work that remains is used with their permission.[1]

Finally, I would like to acknowledge Professor Michael Greenlee, Director of the George R. While Law Library at Concordia University School of Law for his helpful guidance on early drafts of chapters, Professor Jason Dykstra

---

1. As do other books in this series, portions of this book draw on *Oregon Legal Research* by Suzanne Rowe, particularly the introduction to legal research in Chapter 1, the discussion of secondary sources in Chapter 4, the guidance on reading cases in Chapter 11, and the explanation of the national citation manuals in Chapter 13. All of these portions are used with permission.

at Concordia University School of Law, for his editing and proofing of drafts, and Abigail Schwartz, my research assistant, for providing me with her perspective on the updates to this edition as well as editing and proofing drafts of the manuscript.

Tenielle Fordyce-Ruff

Idaho Legal Research

Chapter 1

The Research Process and Legal Analysis

I. Introduction to Idaho Legal Research

If you want to distinguish yourself in the legal field, you need to understand and excel at legal research. Most new law firm associates spend between 40% and 60% of their work hours conducting legal research.[1] Further, law students working at large American firms as summer associates devote between 50% and 100% of their time to legal research.[2]

The fundamentals of legal research are the same in every American jurisdiction, though the details vary. While some variations are minor, others require specialized knowledge of the resources available and the analytical framework resources are used in. This book focuses on the resources and analysis required to be thorough and effective in researching Idaho law. This book provides instruction in conducting research both online and in print, focusing on providing instruction on the most cost effective and efficient resources.

This book also recognizes that while legal research began as a linear process conducted in print, the transition to electronic research has changed the game. With the breadth of information available online, legal research needs no longer be linear. The focus of this book is on presenting a research method that allows researchers to ensure that their research is complete and cost-effective. This book is not designed to be a blueprint of every resource in the law library or

---

1. LexisNexis, Hiring Partners Reveal New Attorney Readiness for Real World Practice 1 (2015), https://www.lexisnexis.com/documents/pdf/20150325064926_large.pdf.
2. LexisNexis, Summer Associates Identify Writing and Legal Research Skills Required on the Job 2 (2016), http://www.lexisnexis.com/documents/pdf/20161109032544_large.pdf.

search engine on the Internet; many resources contain their own detailed explanations in a preface or a "Help" section.

Rather than focusing exclusively on in-depth instruction into the various resources available, this book will provide researchers with a method that they can use on any platform. This book is more like a manual or field guide, introducing the resources needed for each portion of the research process and explaining how to use them. You will benefit most from this text by reading it with your computer open to relevant websites or in the library near the sources being discussed.

II. The Intersection of Legal Research and Legal Analysis

The basic process of legal research is simple. Most online research requires searching particular websites or databases using words likely to appear in the text of relevant documents. For most print resources, researchers begin with an index, find entries that appear relevant, read those sections of the text, and then find out whether more recent information is available.

Legal analysis is interwoven throughout this process, raising challenging questions. With online research, how will you choose relevant words and construct a search most likely to produce the documents you need? In print research, which words will you look up in the index? How will you decide whether an index entry looks promising? When you read the text of a document, how will you determine whether it is relevant to your client's situation? How will you learn whether more recent material changed the law or merely applied it in a new situation?

The answer to each of these questions requires legal analysis. This intersection of research and analysis can make legal research very difficult, especially for the novice. While this book's focus is legal research, it also includes the fundamental aspects of legal analysis required to conduct research competently.

III. Types of Legal Authority

Before researching the law, be clear about the goal of your search. In every research situation, you will want to find constitutional provisions, statutes, administrative rules, and judicial opinions that control your client's situation. In other words, you are searching for primary, mandatory authority.

Table 1-1. Examples of Authority in Idaho Research

	Mandatory Authority	Persuasive Authority
Primary Authority	Idaho Constitution Idaho statutes Idaho administrative rules Idaho Supreme Court cases	Montana Constitution Wyoming statutes Utah administrative rules Washington Supreme Court cases
Secondary Authority	—	Practice guides Treatises Law review articles Legal encyclopedias

Law is often divided along two lines. The first line distinguishes primary authority from secondary authority. *Primary authority* is law produced by government bodies with law-making power. Legislatures write statutes; courts write judicial opinions; and administrative agencies write rules (also called regulations). *Secondary authorities*, in contrast, are materials that are written about the law, generally by practicing attorneys, law professors, or legal editors. Secondary authorities include law practice guides, treatises, law review articles, and legal encyclopedias. These secondary sources are designed to aid researchers in understanding the law and locating primary authority.

Another division is made between mandatory and persuasive authority. *Mandatory authority* is binding on the court that would decide a conflict if the situation were litigated. In a question of Idaho law, mandatory (or binding) authority includes Idaho's constitution, statutes enacted by the Idaho legislature, opinions of the Supreme Court of Idaho,[3] and Idaho administrative rules. *Persuasive authority* is not binding, but may be followed if relevant and well-reasoned. Authority may be merely persuasive if it is from a different jurisdiction or if it is not produced by a law-making body. In a question of Idaho law, examples of persuasive authority include a similar Wyoming statute, an opinion of a Washington state court, and a law review article. Notice in Table 1-1 that persuasive authority may be either primary or secondary authority, while mandatory authority is always primary.

---

3. An opinion from the Court of Appeals is binding on the trial courts if the Supreme Court of Idaho has not addressed the particular topic. *State v. Grist,* 147 Idaho 49, 53, 205 P.3d 1185, 1189 (2009).

Within primary, mandatory authority, there is an interlocking hierarchy of law involving constitutions, statutes, administrative rules, and judicial opinions. The constitution of each state is the supreme law of that state. If a statute is on point, that statute comes next in the hierarchy, followed by administrative rules. Judicial opinions may interpret a statute or rule, but they cannot disregard it. A judicial opinion may, however, decide that a statute violates the constitution or that a rule oversteps its bounds. If there is no constitutional provision, statute, or administrative rule on point, the issue will be controlled by *common law*, also called judge-made law.[4]

IV. Overview of the Research Process

Conducting effective legal research means creating a research strategy and developing a specific research plan for that particular research project. In other words, effective legal research involves following a process. This research process leads to the authority that controls a legal issue as well as to commentary that may help in analyzing new and complex legal matters. Table 1-2 presents the basic research process.

This basic process should be customized for each research project. Consider whether you need to follow all six steps and, if so, in what order. If you are unfamiliar with an area of law, you should follow each step of the process in the order indicated in Table 1-2. Beginning with secondary sources will provide both context for the issues you must research and citations to relevant primary authority. As you gain experience in researching legal questions, you may choose to modify the process. For example, if you know that a statute controls your client's problem, you may choose to begin with that step.

Legal research is not a neat, linear process, however. Instead, each of the six steps is like the spoke of a wheel, leading to the hub—primary, mandatory authority that controls the client's situation. You may start down one path and find that you need to double back to a different step. You may jump back and forth between different steps as your research reveals more about a project. This starting and stopping, or spiraling toward the center, are normal aspects of legal research.

---

4. Common law is derived from judicial decisions, rather than statutes or constitutions. *Black's Law Dictionary* 293 (8th ed. 2004).

Table 1-2. Overview of the Research Process

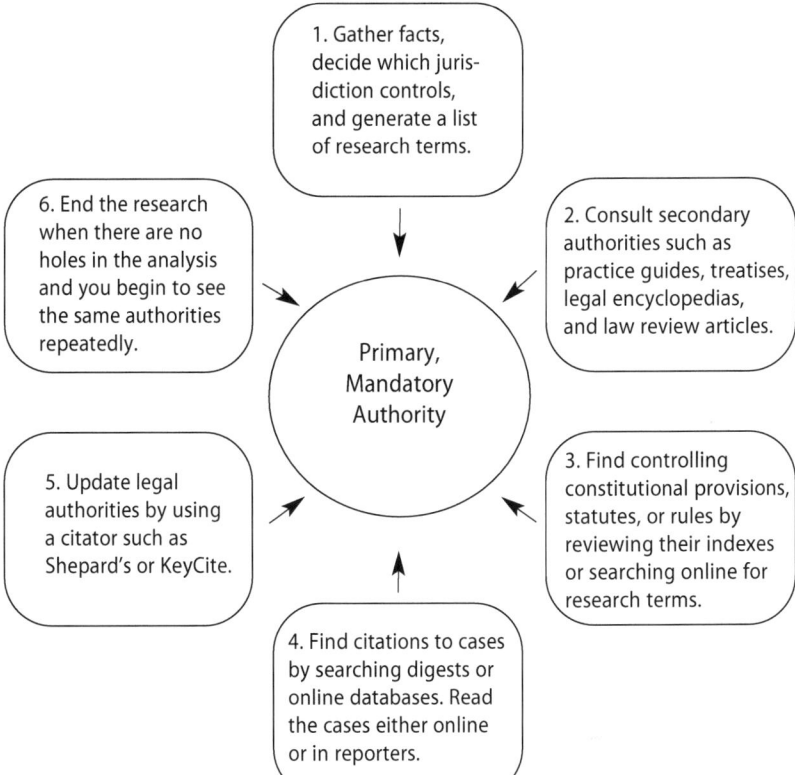

A. Getting Started

Beginning any research project requires four preliminary steps. First, you need to gather facts and understand exactly what you've been asked to research. In practice this can include interviewing the client, reviewing documents, and talking to colleagues. Next, you need to determine which jurisdiction's law controls the issue. Then you need to generate research terms. Finally, you also need to create a research strategy and organize your research results.

B. Research Secondary Authorities

The second step of research is to consult *secondary authorities* such as practice guides, treatises, legal encyclopedias, and law review articles. Secondary authorities explain the law in language that is often easier to understand initially than statutes, cases, or other primary authority. Secondary sources refer to primary authorities, often in extensive footnotes. Thus, research in secondary sources provides helpful background information and citations to primary authorities.

C. Research Enacted Law

The highest primary authority is enacted law, which includes *constitutional provisions*, *statutes*, and *administrative rules*. Constitutions are written by constitutional conventions, statutes are enacted by legislatures, and administrative rules are promulgated by agencies such as the Department of Water Resources.[5]

Researchers find relevant enacted law by searching online databases using research terms or reviewing indexes of books that publish that law. After finding a relevant provision, read it carefully. Also read provisions just before and after it, as several provisions may work in tandem. Then study their annotations for cross-references to additional authorities and explanatory materials.

D. Research Case Law

The next step in the research process requires researching case law. It's likely that the previous two steps will have revealed citations to relevant cases— either in the footnotes of secondary authorities or in the annotations to relevant constitutional provisions, statutes, and administrative rules. Constructing online searches and *topic searching* are also useful ways to find relevant cases. After finding citations to cases, read them in reporters or in online databases. A *reporter* series publishes the full text of cases in a certain jurisdiction or subject area.

E. Update the Law

The next step is to use citators to update the relevant law located through the research process. *Citators* list cases and other sources that have cited a specific authority, allowing a researcher to (1) ensure that an authority has not

---

5. Most first-year research courses concentrate almost exclusively on statutory law. This concentration mirrors the first-year curriculum, which often delays constitutional law and rarely addresses administrative law. In practice, all types of enacted law are critically important and must be considered in each research project.

been repealed, reversed, modified, or otherwise changed and (2) find additional sources that may be relevant to the research project.

F. End Research

One of the most difficult questions in legal research is deciding when to stop researching and begin writing. Often deadlines imposed by the court or a supervisor limit the amount of time spent on a research project. The expense to the client is also a consideration.

Apart from these practical constraints, most legal researchers want to believe that if they search long enough they will find a case or statute or article or *something* that answers the client's legal question clearly and definitively. Sometimes that happens; if you find the answer, you know your research is over. Even without finding a clear answer, when your research in various sources leads back to the same authorities, you can be confident that you have been thorough. As a final checklist, go through each step of the basic research process to ensure you considered each one. Then develop an outline of your analysis to see whether you have sufficient legal support for each point.

If you have worked through the research process and found nothing, it may be that nothing exists. Before reaching that conclusion, expand your research terms and look in a few more secondary sources. Consider whether other jurisdictions may have helpful persuasive authority.

V. Researching the Law — Organization of This Book

The remainder of this book explains how to conduct legal research in a variety of sources. Chapter 2 discusses preparing to research and organizing your research results. Chapter 3 discusses research strategies and the advantages of conducting various research tasks in print or online. That chapter also includes fundamental search techniques for online research. You may prefer to skim those chapters now and refer to them frequently, even though a number of references in them will not become clear until you have read the intervening chapters.

Chapter 4 discusses how to use secondary sources and practice aids. Chapter 5 addresses the Idaho Constitution, which is the highest legal authority in the state. Chapter 6 describes the research process for Idaho statutes, while Chapter 7 covers the legislative process, bill tracking, and legislative history. Chapter 8 briefly covers court rules as well as rules of professional ethics. Chapter 9 addresses administrative law. Chapters 10 and 11 explain judicial decisions. Finally, Chapter 12 explains how to update authorities using citators, and Chapter 13 explains legal citations.

Chapter 2

Preparing to Research and Organization Research Results

I. Preparing to Research

This chapter explores in depth the tasks necessary to complete step 1 of the research process. When beginning any research project, researchers should a) gather facts and determine which jurisdiction's law controls, b) generate research terms, c) plan a research strategy, and d) create an organizational system for taking research and analytical notes.

A. Gathering Facts and Determining Jurisdiction

Before ever cracking a book or opening a search engine, you should stop to identify exactly what you've been asked to research. The first step in any research process is to gather the facts of the client's situation. In law practice, gathering facts may include interviewing the client, reviewing documents, and talking to colleagues who are also working for the client.

Make sure you understand the answer to the questions listed in Table 2-1,[1] and you will be well on your way to understanding what you need to accomplish to be successful in your legal research project.

- **Are there any materials related to this case that I may review?**

Always ask to see the client's file, so you can develop familiarity with both the facts and key legal concepts. Even if you are researching a discrete legal

---

1. These questions were adapted from Hollee Schwartz Temple, *West Virginia Legal Research* 7–8 (2d ed. 2018).

Table 2-1. Preliminary Research Questions

- Are there any materials related to this case that I may review?
- What is the expected timeline for this project?
- What is the expected final work product?
- Are there any specialized resources you would recommend?
- What else do I need to know?
- What jurisdictions should I pursue?

issue, reviewing the file can help you generate search terms and understand the issues before you dive into the details.

• What is the expected timeline for this project?

While a novice researcher can take longer than the supervising attorney expects to conduct research, make sure you understand the general expectations before you get started. This way, if you find that you can't complete the project in the expected timeframe, even though you are diligently researching, you can alert the supervisor.

• What is the expected final work product?

Not every legal research project will result in a full-blown appellate brief. Sometimes a supervisor is hoping for a research memo summarizing leading cases; other times she might want a concise email with cases attached. Confirm the final work product expectations before you begin.

• Are there any specialized resources you would recommend?

Specialized materials, like those developed for Continuing Legal Education programs (discussed in Chapter 4), often provide practical information that is hard to locate in more traditional legal resources. If you are working on a narrow legal issue (often times, the more local an issue, the narrower), be sure to ask a supervisor or librarian whether there are any recently published materials that address the issue.

• What else do I need to know?

As you are gathering this preliminary information, ask the supervising attorney if there are any questions that you should have asked but didn't. Because

- **What jurisdictions should I pursue?**

  An early question that arises for any research project is which jurisdiction's law controls the issue. This book assumes that the client's situation is controlled by Idaho law, but in practice you must determine which law (e.g., federal, state, and which circuits or states specifically) will apply to the research project before you begin. You should also confirm whether your supervisor wants you to limit your research to a particular jurisdiction. (For example, if Idaho case law does not produce any mandatory authority on the issue, would your supervisor like you to search in other state courts?)

B. Generating Research Terms

After gathering facts and determining the jurisdiction, generate a list of *research terms*. You will use these terms to create online searches, to review indexes, and to scan tables of contents. To ensure you are thorough in beginning a research project, you will need a comprehensive list of words, terms, and phrases that may lead to law on point. These may be legal terms or common words that describe the client's situation. The items on this list are *research terms*.

Organized brainstorming is the best way to compile a comprehensive list of research terms. Some researchers ask the journalistic questions: Who? What? How? Why? When? Where? Others use a mnemonic device like TARPP, which stands for Things, Actions, Remedies, People, and Places. Whether you use one of these suggestions or develop your own method, generate a broad range of research terms regarding the facts, issues, and desired solutions of the client's situation. Include in the list both specific and general words. Try to think of synonyms and antonyms for each term since at this point you are uncertain which terms an index or online document may include. Using a legal dictionary or thesaurus may also generate additional terms.

As an example, assume you are working for a defense attorney who was recently assigned to a theft case. Three nights ago, the client found a wallet in an alley that contained $127 in one pocket and a credit card and debit card in another pocket she did not notice. Although the wallet also contained the owner's identification, the client did not attempt to return it. She has been charged with grand theft, a felony. You have been asked to determine if there is a good argument for limiting the charge to petit theft, a misdemeanor, based

Table 2-2. Generating Research Terms

Journalistic Approach	
Who:	Thief, robber
What:	Theft, grand theft, petit theft, wallet, credit card, debit card, cash
How:	Found, discovered, failed to return
Why:	Theft, stealing, stolen goods
When:	Nighttime
Where:	Alley, street, public street
TARPP Approach	
Things:	Wallet, credit card, debit card, cash
Actions:	Theft, damages, crime, failure to return
Remedies:	Grand theft, petit theft, incarceration, felony, misdemeanor
People:	Thief, wallet owner
Places:	Alley, street, public street

on the fact that she was unaware that the wallet contained the credit and debit cards. Table 2-2 provides examples of research terms you might use to begin work on this project.

The goal of initial brainstorming is to produce as many terms as possible. When you begin researching, use those terms that appear on the list most often or that seem most important. As the project progresses, you will learn new research terms to include in the list and decide to take others off. For example, a secondary source may refer to a *term of art*, a word or phrase that has special meaning in a particular area of law. Later in the research, a new case may provide insight into the key words judges tend to use in discussing this topic. These terms and words need to be added to the list. You should review the list periodically to help refine your research. If an online search produces far too many results, review the list for more specific search terms. On the other hand, if the terms you use initially produce no hits, review the list for alternative, more general terms.

C. Planning a Research Strategy

The research process presented in Chapter 1 contains six steps: (1) understand the scope of the project, generate a list of *research terms*, and prepare a research strategy; (2) consult *secondary sources* and practice aids; (3) find controlling *constitutional provisions*, *statutes*, or *administrative rules*; (4) research

Table 2-3. Planning a Research Strategy

1. Consider the research process you want to follow for the project.
2. Determine which providers to search for each step in the process.
3. Create cost effective searches for each step in the research process.
4. Select the search techniques to use in each provider.

judicial opinions; (5) *update* your legal authorities with a citator; and (6) *end* your research when you have no holes in your analysis and when you begin seeing the same authorities repeatedly. Table 2-3 outlines how to implement the research process into your research strategy and the implementation is explained below.

1. Which Process?

In the initial phases, planning a research strategy means considering the six fundamental research steps and then deciding where to begin and how to proceed. Your decision will vary for each project. When researching an unfamiliar area of law, you will likely be more successful beginning with secondary sources. If you are familiar with an area of statutory law from previous work, your research may be more effective if you go directly to an annotated code. If you are working for another attorney who gives you a citation to a case she knows is relevant, you may want to begin by Shepardizing or KeyCiting the case, discussed in greater detail in Chapter 12, or leveraging topic connectivity as discussed in Chapter 11. Both steps may quickly provide more cases on point. Finally, if you know that the issue is controlled by common law, you may feel comfortable not researching statutory or constitutional provisions or spending very little time in those areas. As you consider this phase of research, write a quick strategy for your particular project, listing the research steps you will take in the order you have chosen.

Although your research strategy will be written in a series of discrete steps, remember that the research process is not necessarily linear. Efficient research sometimes requires jumping back and forth between the different spokes of the research wheel. For example, a secondary source may cite a relevant case that you decide to read immediately, not two steps later. Updating may reveal more cases that you need to read, or it may uncover a new law review article that is on point. As you learn more about a project, you may want to review whether your earlier research was effective, particularly with the research terms used. Even as you begin writing, you may need to do more research if new issues arise or if you need more support for an argument. Circling back and skipping forward are normal aspects of legal research. Reviewing your research strategy frequently will ensure that you do not inadvertently forget a fundamental research step.

2. Determine Which Provider to Search

Remember at this stage that your goal is to find all the relevant legal authority. You also need to ensure that the materials you find are accurate and to take into consideration the structure of legal information. Thus, when determining which online provider to use in your research process, be realistic about how effectively and efficiently your search can produce material that is accurate and authoritative.

- *Is this Authoritative?*

Documents written by a governmental body (courts, legislatures, and administrative agencies) are "the law." Articles and treatises written by recognized experts in a field are not binding, but they can be very persuasive and are often authoritative. To learn what resources a particular site contains and the dates of coverage, look for a "+" or "i" or "?" icon.

- *Is this Official?*

Look for a note on government websites indicating whether its contents are official or authenticated. Often, the print versions of statutes are the official versions, while increasingly a government's online version of administrative rules will be official, as is the case in Idaho.

- *Is this Comprehensive?*

Most recent material is available on many websites, but some historical material and some important secondary materials may be available only on limited websites or in print.

- *What Context is Provided?*

Increasingly, online sources provide a table of contents and other tools that provide context for the reading. These sources are valuable because they aid understanding.

- **Is this Annotated or Topically Connected?**

While many sites will provide the text of a case or statute, the more helpful research sites will also provide annotations or links to related materials.

- **Is this Current?**

Check both to see how recent the available material is and to ensure that the online source covers the period of time relevant to your research (especially when doing historical work). Some online sources are no more current than their print counterparts, and websites may contain outdated material.

- **Is this Cost Effective?**

The best way to find accurate and authoritative material online is by using highly regarded and dependable sites. Some examples of established, reputable online research sites include less expensive, but less robust, commercial sites, such as Casemaker; free online providers like Google Scholar; free government websites; and free university and law school library websites Additionally, expensive platforms provided by Lexis and Westlaw are also established and reputable. Chapter 3 provides more detail about selecting online sources for legal research.

Online sources provided by governments and universities are free and highly reliable. If the document you need is available on a free site, look for it there rather than using a costly commercial provider. Online commercial services can be very expensive. A single research project, poorly conceived and sloppily done, can cost hundreds or even thousands of dollars on a subscription service. On the other hand, a well-done search in a commercial provider's extensive database could be worth the cost. Check the billing practices in your office before using commercial online sources. Also, be sure you know your office's policy regarding the printing of documents from commercial service websites, which often brings extra charges.

3. Creating Effective Searches

Next, you need to take your research terms and create searches that are likely to yield the results you need. Most legal research is conducted online, using various databases. Therefore, you need to pay careful attention to the ways the various online providers interpret searches. For instance, how does this provider interpret a space? Does the provider allow you to type a simple question? Does the provider work better if you use terms and connectors specific to it?

If your initial search yields too many results, don't start over right away. Instead, determine if the terms and connectors you used could be narrowed and review the list for additional search terms to help you create a narrower search. If your initial search yields too few results, review your list for more general terms, make the search broader by removing terms and connectors or use a natural language search.

4. Select Search Techniques

Most websites can be searched using at least one of several techniques: searching by citation, searching with terms and connectors, searching with natural language, or searching a table of contents or index. Each online provider has a different interface and a different method of retrieving information. While there are fundamental similarities in the search algorithms for all the providers, the websites are constantly being revised and updated. As such, look for "Help" link to learn more about the search techniques for a particular provider. Chapter 3 provides more detail about various online search techniques.

II. Keeping Track of Research Results

A. Research Notes

As you conduct research, take careful notes. Taking notes on your research strategy (the process you wrote out at the beginning of the project) can help you avoid duplicating steps, especially if you have to interrupt your research for a notable length of time.

For each new resource, make notes that summarize your work in that resource. For print research, include the volumes you used, the indexes or tables you reviewed, the terms you searched for, and the search results. For online research, include the site, the specific database or link, and the searches that you entered. Note the date that you performed each search. When working with Lexis and Westlaw, use their "History" and "Research Trail" functions to keep track of online searches. Keep track of both successful and unsuccessful research terms and searches so that you do not inadvertently repeat these same steps later, or so you can revisit a "dead end" that later becomes relevant.

B. Analytical Notes

In addition to taking research notes, take analytical notes. These notes provide a basis for organizing your thoughts and preparing your arguments. Analytical notes do not have to be formal or typed; in fact, you might waste valuable time by following too much structure or stopping to type notes. Take analytical notes on all relevant secondary sources, enacted law, cases, and updating.

Write a short summary for each secondary source you consult. Begin the summary with the title, author, and other citation information for the source. In your own words, summarize the relevant analysis in the source, including references to specific pages. Try to include a few sentences—written in your own words—explaining how this source relates to your research. Does it give the background of a statute? Does it trace the development of a line of cases? Does it criticize the law in your jurisdiction? Does it suggest a novel approach to your problem? Additionally, note any references to primary authorities that may be on point, and include these in a list of primary authorities (explained below).

Notes on enacted laws (constitutional provisions, statutes, and administrative rules) should include both the actual language that was enacted and your outline of it. Because the exact words of enacted laws are so important, you should print or copy the text of these provisions. Be sure to refer to the definition sections of statutes; where important terms are not defined, make a note to look for judicial definitions. Also be sure to read statutes or regulations that are cross-referenced. As noted in Chapter 6 on statutes, Chapter 8 on Court Rules, and Chapter 9 on administrative law, to fully understand a complex statute or rule, you should outline it. Highlighting language is sufficient only if the statute or rule is very short and clear.

If a case is relevant, brief it. The brief does not have to follow any formal style. Instead, the brief for each case should be a set of notes that highlight the key aspects of the case that are relevant for your research problem. You may choose to write this brief on your computer. You might prefer to write your brief on your legal pad or create an index card. Each case brief should include the case's citation, the relevant facts, the holding and the court's reasoning, pinpoint pages on which critical information appears, and your thoughts on the case.

Be sure to note on each brief the date that you updated each case with either KeyCite or Shepard's. Printing lists of citing references is an easy and efficient way to compare new citations with other lists of relevant authorities to avoid duplication.

Do not underestimate the learning process that occurs while taking analytical notes. Deciding what is important enough to include in notes and expressing those ideas in your own words will increase your understanding of the legal issues involved. Pressing the "Print" key and highlighting do not provide this same analytical advantage.

III. Organizing Research Results

Legal research often produces many documents that must be organized along with your notes. At the outset, you must determine whether to organize your research results online or in print. Even in online research, you may want to print key documents to ensure careful reading and comprehension. Thus, you need to develop methods of keeping documents organized and sorting out your analysis.

If you work better with printed sources, you will likely need a three-ring binder or a set of files in which you keep hard copies of the most important authorities. Using tabs can keep you from flipping endlessly through documents. Additionally, both Lexis and Westlaw allow you to organize your online research in *folders*.

Create a list of primary sources that contains the name and citation for all the primary authorities that you need to read. Throughout your research, as you come across a potentially relevant authority, include it on the list. This method will allow you to maintain your train of thought with one resource while ensuring that you keep track of important cites to check later. After creating a list that includes a number of sources, check for duplicates before reading the authorities.

Once you have selected a number of relevant authorities, choose an organizational scheme for reading them carefully in groups. If there is a constitutional provision, statute, or rule on point, begin by reading it carefully, then move to reading cases that interpret the provision. One approach is to read cases in chronological order, so that you see the development of the law over time. This may be time consuming for causes of action that have existed for many years. Except for historical research, impose an artificial cut-off of twenty or thirty years in the past, so that you put your effort into reading recent law. The opposite approach works in many situations: by beginning with the recent cases, you avoid spending time learning old law that has been revised or superseded.

While reading relevant authorities, pay attention to parts that you may have skipped earlier while skimming during the research process. Read carefully the definitions in statutes. Be sure you understand the procedural posture of each case, since this affects the standard of review applied. Also be sure that you understand the facts of cases. Drawing a time line or a chart of the relationships between the parties may be helpful. As you read through the case, cross out portions dealing with legal issues that are not relevant to your client's problem. If you decide that the case is actually not important, mark that on the first page so that you will not waste time reading it again.

When researching several issues or related claims, consider them one at a time. In this instance, you may have several lists of primary authorities, one for each claim you are researching. You may want to create a different section in your binder for each claim.

If you prefer to work with online documents both Westlaw and Lexis allow you to keep track of your research and take notes on their platforms. Your searches will be saved under the "History" links. You can organize your research by saving specific documents in "Folders" that you can create for each project. Both services also allow you to highlight and annotate documents and to share your work with others. While these tools serve experienced researchers well, until you are an experienced researcher you should also keep notes in print. Many researchers work more efficiently flipping through a binder or shuffling through a stack of cases than they do scrolling through online files.

IV. Outlining the Analysis

Because the most effective research often occurs in conjunction with the analysis of your particular project, try to develop an outline that addresses your client's problem as soon as you can. If outlining feels too restrictive, you may benefit from a chart that organizes all the primary authority by issue or element, such as in Table 2-4, following the typical legal analysis format of Conclusion-Rule-Explanation-Application-Conclusion (CREAC). In the "Rule" portion, explain only the legal rule. In the "Explanation" portion, discuss the relevant facts and the court's reasoning from the cases. Apply the case to your client's problem and reach a conclusion. (Remember that a thorough legal analysis will synthesize these portions, rather than addressing each case individually.)

Your first analytical outline or chart may be based on information in a secondary source, the requirements of a statute, or the elements of a common law claim. It will become more sophisticated and detailed as you conduct your research. Recognize that you cannot reread every case or statute in its entirety each time you need to include it in your outline; instead, refer to your notes and briefs to find the key ideas supporting each step in your analysis.

Table 2-4. Sample Analysis Chart

Client's Facts: Adjacent to the client's property is a square parcel of land surrounded by a fence that was standing when she purchased the property. Ownership of the parcel is uncertain, but she has been using this parcel as her property and her neighbors have treated it as her property for twenty-three years.

Research Question: Can the client establish ownership of the adjacent, fenced parcel?

Legal Issue: Can ownership be established through boundary by agreement?

Case	Rule	Rule Explanation	Application to Client and Conclusion
a. *Cox v. Clanton*, 137 Idaho 492, 50 P.3d 987 (2002).	Two elements: (1) an uncertain or disputed boundary and (2) a subsequent agreement fixing the boundary.	Although neighbors disputed true boundary line, evidence showed purpose of fence was not to establish boundary, but to contain cattle.	Neighbors don't dispute client's ownership; original purpose of fence unknown.
b. *Johnson v. Newport*, 131 Idaho 521, 960 P.2d 742 (1998).	Long established fence treated as boundary creates presumption of boundary by agreement.	Although no evidence of why fence erected, treated as boundary for many years.	Most likely can prove boundary by agreement because fence was erected more than twenty years ago.
c. *Luce v. Marble*, 142 Idaho 264, 127 P.3d 167 (2005).	Specific facts of case can overcome presumption created by longstanding fence treated as boundary.	Irregular shape of fenced parcel overcomes presumption of boundary by agreement created by longstanding fence treated as a boundary.	Parcel is regularly shaped, so client should be able to use presumption to establish ownership.
d. *Griffel v. Reynolds*, 136 Idaho 397, 34 P.3d 1080 (2001).	An agreement can be implied from the surrounding circumstances and conduct of the landowners.	Court implied boundary by agreement from evidence parties had used farming lines as boundary for more than twenty years.	Client can likely imply an agreement from longstanding usage and neighbors' conduct.

The outline or chart should enable you to synthesize the law, apply the law to your client's facts, and reach a conclusion on the desired outcome. Applying the law to your client's facts may lead you to research issues that may not be apparent in a merely theoretical discussion of the law.

Chapter 3

Research Techniques

While the majority of legal research is conducted online, using a "google" search technique is unlikely to lead to fruitful results. Instead, understanding how legal information is structured as well as what information you have at the beginning of a search will help you create a better research strategy and employ efficient, cost-effective research.

I. The Structure of Legal Information

Legal research is about the search for all of the primary, mandatory authority dealing with a specific legal issue. While there has been a drastic increase in the number of resources that will provide a researcher with primary authority, the publishers of these various resources recognize the goal of legal research. To that end, various sources and finding tools are organized to help legal researchers meet their goal. Recognizing the organization underpinning legal information can help you as you plan your search.

First, legal information is organized topically. Because you are searching for all of the law on a particular topic, legal publishers have collected and organized their publications topically to allow you to simplify your search. For instance, statutes and regulations are organized by subject and then codified. Digests, finding tools to locate case law, are also organized topically. Therefore, researchers needing to find all the law related to adverse possession could turn to the chapter in the Idaho Code dealing with that topic to find the applicable statutes and turn to the volume in the Idaho digest dealing with that topic to find case law.

Second, the law is published chronologically. All enacted law and all cases are published in the order in which they were produced. While publishers eventually organize legal materials topically, they will also publish authorities as they are produced. This helps researches stay abreast of the most recent changes to the law. It also helps the researcher conduct historical research, as older authority isn't removed. Instead, it remains static and legal researchers can find what the law was at any point in the past.

Finally, legal resources are connected. Editors add citations from one publication to another when the publication addresses the same legal issue. This connectivity helps researchers locate all of the law that applies to the particular legal issue. For instance, with finding tools, researchers can then use the citations to locate primary authority or additional secondary authority.

II. Online Legal Research Sources

The first step in online legal research is to determine where to conduct your search. Many online tools can be used; some are highly sophisticated in their search capacity while others require that the researcher be very precise in using search terms. Chapter 2 addressed the questions you should ask when determining which provider to search. Table 3-1 lists examples of established, reputable online research sites for Idaho materials. For each site, look for a link such as "Help" or "Searching Hints" to provide information about finding material on that site. Some sites also offer online tutorials to introduce their resources and search processes; the information they provide can help you better determine whether to use that service for a particular research project.

A. Government and University Websites

Government entities and universities generally provide access to their website information for free. These sites may contain less information than is available from the commercial providers, and the search engines on these sites tend to be less sophisticated. The amount of information available on these sites, however, is increasing, making them more useful research tools. Given that they are free, they are almost always worth exploring.

Like other states, Idaho maintains its own websites for its primary authority. Although the print versions are the "official" authority, the online versions are useful for research. The primary limitation to these sites is that material may be available only for recent years.

In addition, a number of universities provide information and contain links to valuable Internet sites. Both the Concordia University School of Law Library and the University of Idaho College of Law Library are useful sites for Idaho researchers. Cornell Law School's Legal Information Institute and Washburn University School of Law's "WashLaw" can also help researchers as the Idaho

Table 3-1. Online Research Websites

Name	Web Address	Free or Commercial
Bloomberg Law	bloomberglaw.com	Commercial
Casemaker	isb.idaho.gov	Free to members of the Idaho State Bar
Concordia University School of Law Library	law.cu-portland.edu/library/databases	Free
Cornell University Law School Legal Information Institute	law.cornell.edu	Free
Google Scholar	scholar.google.com	Free
FindLaw	findlaw.com	Free
Idaho State Judiciary	isc.idaho.gov	Free
Idaho Legislature	legislature.idaho.gov	Free
Idaho Secretary of State	idsos.state.id.us	Free
Idaho State Law Library	isll.idaho.gov	Free
Lexis Advance	lexis.com	Commercial
Loislaw	loislaw.com	Commercial
University of Idaho College of Law Library	law.uidaho.edu	Free
VersusLaw	versuslaw.com	Commercial
WashLaw (Washburn University School of Law)	washlaw.edu	Free
Westlaw Edge	westlaw.com	Commercial

portions of those websites list links to Idaho cases, statutes, administrative materials, and more. A similar "gateway" site is FindLaw.

B. Other Commercial and Free Providers

Lexis and Westlaw are the largest commercial providers of computerized legal research; they provide the most documents and have the most advanced search techniques. Both have reputations for accurate material and user-friendly search techniques. They provide extensive coverage of primary and secondary authority.

Other commercial providers of legal materials include Bloomberg Law, Casemaker, Loislaw, and VersusLaw. They tend to be less expensive than Lexis and Westlaw, but they also provide less extensive coverage. Nonetheless, these services might suit your needs for a particular research project. Some of these providers allow you to search their sites as a visitor before deciding whether to subscribe to their services. Casemaker is provided to all Idaho State Bar members. Each of these services provides searchable databases for primary authorities in Idaho, and each has a form of a citator.

Google Scholar provides free materials, including state and federal cases and law review articles. It also has a rudimentary citator. It doesn't currently include statutes, regulations, or other legal documents.

No matter which provider you chose for a research project, each is likely to have its own unique search techniques and commands. Make sure to use the "Help" or "Tips" link when using an unfamiliar service to ensure that you're using a search likely to yield results.

III. Conducting Research Using Lexis, Westlaw, and Other Services

Each website has a different method for retrieving information, though all tend to follow the same algorithms. Because most websites are constantly being revised and because their search methods change over time, only general information is possible in an overview such as this book. The following explanations are primarily for Lexis and Westlaw, though much of the information should be easily applicable to other online sources.

The world of online legal researching is quickly changing. Providers introduce new products to facilitate legal research, hoping to make it easier for the researcher to access the primary and secondary sources discussed throughout this book. These providers are not creating new sources of law. Therefore, researchers who are unfamiliar with a particular electronic research platform should read or view any tutorials provided by the service on how to conduct research using that platform. Bear in mind, however, that no matter how you are researching, what you are looking for remains the same.

The novice researcher must be careful to avoid becoming overwhelmed by the large number of results uncovered through an electronic search. Like the researcher entering a physical law library, the researcher should determine what types of sources will most likely lead to the information sought and consult those sources first. The researcher should also use filters to narrow results; the goal is rarely to have read everything ever written on a subject in every jurisdiction, but instead to locate information relevant to the issue on which the researcher is working.

Platforms like Lexis and Westlaw provide efficient tools for saving and organizing research. Documents can be saved in electronic folders, and the researcher can take notes on documents and highlight relevant passages on the electronic version of the documents. Folders can be shared with others working on the same project. The platforms also keep track of the researcher's prior searches so that research can be done more efficiently with little duplication or backtracking.

Both Lexis and Westlaw currently allow a researcher to begin researching by entering a citation, table of contents search, natural language search, terms-and-connectors search, and topic search.

A. Find by Citation

When you have a citation to a case, statute, article, or other legal source, retrieving that document online is as simple as typing the citation into the search box on the appropriate screen. Typing *Idaho Code 5-210* into Westlaw leads to the state statute narrowing the methods by which a person can claim oral title to real property. Likewise, typing *142 Idaho 264* into Lexis retrieves the 2005 case of *Luce v. Marble* where the Idaho Supreme Court applies the requirements of Idaho Code § 5-210 to a specific factual situation. Note that many online providers list acceptable citation formats for retrieving documents, and these forms vary from provider to provider.

The advantage to starting your search by entering a known citation comes from the connectivity of legal information. Editors add citations to other sources that address the same legal topics for each document, allowing researchers to expand their research results quickly.

B. Table of Contents Searching

Both Lexis and Westlaw, and an increasing number of other providers, provide table of contents. These tables list the major segments of a document or set of documents. For example, just as a book's table of contents lists all the chapters in order, the Idaho Code has a table of contents that lists all of the statutes in numerical order. An online table of contents often lists major headings on the initial screen and subheadings may be accessed by clicking on the heading or a symbol next to the heading.

For example, in a divorce dispute over whether a marriage settlement agreement is valid, you could open the table of contents for Idaho statutes on Lexis, Westlaw, or the Idaho Legislature's website and scan the list of titles until you found "Domestic Relations." Clicking on that link would open the list of chapters under that title, including Chapter 9 on "Husband and Wife — Property."

Table of contents searching provides researchers with two advantages. First, you can see how the issues and subtopics in an area of law are related. Second, you can quickly find relevant portions or documents or databases.

C. Using Search Terms

1. Natural Language Searching

Natural language searching allows you to use a simple word, phrase, or question to search. The providers then produce a list of results and rank the results. On providers like Lexis and Westlaw, these types of searches can produce excellent results; on less sophisticated providers, these types of searches can produce more limited results.

On Lexis and Westlaw you begin the search by entering your terms into the main search bar. Both services have algorithms that search for both the exact natural language search you used as well as related terms. While you can enter your search from the main search bar, you might want to limit the results you will retrieve. You can limit by the type of law addressed in the document (e.g. contracts or criminal law), by category of documents (e.g. cases or regulations), or by jurisdiction (e.g. Idaho or the Ninth Circuit). You can also narrow results after the search by using filters such as restricting the search by court or date.

Other providers might not allow you to use natural language searching. Even if it is available, it is not a comprehensive way to search less sophisticated providers. Consider using natural language searching to begin researching on these services, then using terms-and-connectors or topic searching to refine your searching.

No matter which provider you're using, natural language searching can produce many results that aren't relevant to your research. There are a few reasons for this. First, some providers set natural language searches to produce a certain number of results, but that doesn't mean that every document produced is relevant. Second, you might not have crafted the search carefully enough. Finally, there might not be any more relevant results. Nevertheless, even if the first screen of results doesn't look promising, skim through numerous results as a relevant document could appear later in the list.

Natural language searching provides some advantages: it allows you to use simple words or phrases instead of legal terms and allows the algorithm to decide which words are critical, where the words should appear in relation to

3 · RESEARCH TECHNIQUES

Table 3-2. Formulating Effective Terms-and-Connectors Searches

1. Generate search terms and modify them using expanders and placeholders.
2. Add connectors.
3. Choose databases to search.
4. Use segments or fields to restrict the search.
5. Refine the search as needed based on results.

one another, and how often they should appear in the document. Once you have retrieved a relevant result, you can use other research methods to find more relevant documents. It also allows you to quickly search for terms of art, like "boundary by agreement," or less common issues, like "specific performance."

2. Terms-and-Connectors Searching

Terms-and-connectors searching allows you to create more precise searches and to dictate where search terms are in relation to each other in a document by using Boolean connectors.[1] These connectors enable you to more accurately control what the computer searches for. Advantages to using terms-and-connectors searches are that the results are more precise and more likely to be complete. Table 3-2 outlines the steps for formulating an effective terms-and-connectors search.

- *Generate and Modify Search Terms*

Use the suggestions in Chapter 2 to generate a comprehensive list of research terms. Next, modify the terms with expanders and placeholders. These allow the search engine to find variations of your terms. Expanders are used to expand your term beyond its root; the most common expander is the exclamation point. Placeholders serve to replace a single letter, and the most common are the asterisk or question mark. Use a placeholder when you aren't sure what form of a word is used or you aren't sure of the spelling. For example, using the term *function!* would retrieve function, functional, functionality, and functionary. Using the terms *function*** would eliminate functionality

---

1. George Boole was a British mathematician. The Boolean connectors that carry his name dictate the logical relationship of search terms to each other.

Table 3-3. Boolean Expanders, Placeholders, and Connectors

Goal	Lexis	Westlaw
To find alternative terms anywhere in the document	or	or blank space
To find both terms anywhere in the document	and &	and &
To find both terms within a particular distance from each other	/p = in 1 paragraph /s = in 1 sentence /n = within *n* words	/p = in 1 paragraph /s = in 1 sentence /n = within *n* words
To find terms used as a phrase	leave a blank space between each word of the phrase	put the phrase in quotation marks
To control the hierarchy of searching	parentheses	parentheses
To exclude terms	and not	but not %
To extend the end of a term	! *	!
To hold the place of letters in a term	?	*

(trademark term) and functionary (public employee) but retain function and functional.

- *Add Connectors*

Connectors are used to determine where in a document the terms appear in relation to each other. To use terms-and-connectors searching effectively, think of the ideal document you would like to find and try to imagine where your search terms would be located in relation to each other within that document. Would they be in the same sentence? The same paragraph? Even on unsophisticated services using a rudimentary terms-and-connectors search can narrow the results to those much more likely to be relevant to your research problem. Table 3-3 summarizes the most common expanders, placeholders, and connectors.

Understanding and using connectors effectively is critical to finding relevant research results. Consider an example search designed to determine whether a contract containing a covenant not to compete is enforceable against a former employee.

EXAMPLE: Searching for *(covenant or contract) /p (noncompetition or "restraint of trade" or compet!) /p employ!*, the computer will look for:

- either the term *covenant* or *contract*

- within the same paragraph as the term *noncompetition* or *restraint of trade* or variations of *competition, compete, competitor*

- and also in that paragraph variations of *employ, employee, employer, employment.*

Misuse of connectors can produce bizarre search results. If, instead of "/p" in the example above, the researcher used the "or" connector, the results could include (1) a case in which former spies sued the federal government for failing to adhere to a secret *contract*, (2) a case determining whether an implied *covenant* can be read into an oil and gas lease, and (3) a case dismissing a beer importer's unfair *competition* claim. As another example, the term *compet!* retrieves not only cases about *competition, compete,* and *competitor,* but also cases on a criminal defendant's *competency* to stand trial. To eliminate these cases, use the exclusion connector "but not" or "and not."

- **Choose Databases**

Your research is most likely to be efficient and cost effective, as well as return relevant results, if you search the smallest subset of documents. Many providers also default to allow searching in all the documents available. Thus, beginning by entering a terms-and-connectors search in the main search box could produce a large number of documents that aren't mandatory or primary authority.

To conduct an effective search, begin instead by selecting the database that is the most likely to produce the subset of documents that will answer your research question. These types of searches are more likely to produce mandatory, primary authority and are more likely to be cost effective as searches in smaller databases are typically less expensive than searches in large ones. Only if your initial search in a smaller database produces no relevant result should you consider using a larger database.

Most providers have directories that allow you to search through the list of databases available. Look for a symbol such as "i" next to the name of the database to find information about its scope.

- ***Restrict the Search Using Fields and Segments***

Terms-and-connectors searches typically ask the provider to search the full text of documents to look for exact matches, but Lexis and Westlaw allow you to restrict the terms-and-connectors searches to particular parts of documents. For instance, you can search dates, authors, or courts. On Lexis they are called "Segments"; on Westlaw these are called "Fields." This type of searching can be particularly helpful in some instances. For instance, if you're searching for a secondary source by Tenielle Fordyce-Ruff, using that name in the segment or field for the author would yield only results that she wrote; it would exclude the results where "Tenielle Fordyce-Ruff" appears in a footnote or is mentioned in the text. Likewise, if you restrict a search to the synopsis or syllabi, the search will include only results where your term is at issue.

- ***Refine or Broaden the Search***

If your search produces too few results, you will need to broaden the search. For instance, you may need to search for your terms in the same paragraph instead of the same sentence, or you may need to choose a larger database. You might also need to use more general search terms, such as *marriage contract* instead of *premarital agreement*.

If your search produces too many results, you will need to refine your search. Begin by using more specific search terms, more restrictive connectors, or searching a smaller database.

D. Topic Searching

Both Lexis and Westlaw have tools for topic searching. The most user-friendly of these tools allow the researcher to begin with a list of broad areas of law and narrow the topic by clicking through successive lists. On Lexis this tool is found under the "Browse" tab on the home screen. On Westlaw, the tool is called "Key Number," which is available under "Content types" on the home screen.

As an example, to find cases on the validity of marriage settlement agreements using the West Key Number System, you might begin by clicking on "Divorce," in the broad list, then selecting successively "Spousal Support, Allowances, and Disposition of Property" and "Allocation of Property and Liabilities." Once you have narrowed the topic sufficiently and selected a jurisdiction, the database will retrieve documents on point. As with natural language searching, topic searching may be useful as a starting point, but it is unlikely to produce a comprehensive list of authorities.

IV. Conducting Research in Print

While a vast quantity of information is available online, not all legal material is available there. And even when documents are available both online and in print, using print resources may be more effective or efficient in some instances. Searching in a library might be more cost effective because the library has already paid for the resource. Searching in a print resource might be more efficient because the organization of the source might be more apparent and help you more quickly see how the various topics in the law are related.

When searching in a library, begin by searching the online catalog or asking a reference librarian to suggest specific resources. Once you've found a print resource look at the source's table of contents and index for your research terms.[2] With index searching, spend several minutes looking for all of your research terms and noting the relevant pages or sections of the source that contains your terms. This will ensure that you begin in the most relevant portion of the source, not just the one you encountered first. It will also help you see if the index contains cross-references that could be useful.

---

2. The index is an alphabetical listing of topics contained in a source. For single volumes, it is typically after the text. For multi-volume series, the index may be a separate volume or separate indexes may be provided for each topic.

Chapter 4

Secondary Sources and Practice Aids

I. Introduction

The ultimate goal of any research project is to find mandatory authority, but in some instances the search for that authority will be easier if you begin your research in a secondary source. When researching in an unfamiliar area of law, for instance, the second step of the research process should be *secondary sources*, which include a wide range of books, articles, encyclopedias, practice aids, and other sources. Sources are deemed "secondary" because they are written by law professors, practicing attorneys, legal editors, and even law students; in contrast, "primary" authority is written by legislatures, courts, and administrative agencies. These sources, however, can be valuable to researchers in four instances.

First, secondary sources can provide helpful background information when you are researching an area of the law you are unfamiliar with. For example, if you are working on a case that involves an unfamiliar area of administrative law, you might benefit from consulting a secondary source that explains administrative law broadly and provides context for your specific legal question. Having that context will make it easier for you to generate good search terms that will lead you to primary authorities, and it will help you understand those primary authorities when you begin to read them. A secondary source may provide an overview of the pertinent issues, aiding in the analysis of the legal problem. The text of a secondary source will also likely explain unfamiliar terminology and concepts, making it possible to develop a more effective list of research terms.

Next, secondary sources often provide a shortcut to researching primary authority by including numerous references to cases, statutes, and rules. Third, secondary sources can be a useful tool when you are researching an area of the law that is new or not well-developed. If there is little primary authority to base your answer on, the commentary in secondary authorities could become crucial to your ability to analyze the legal question. Finally, secondary sources can help you sort through the authorities you find, especially if you have found a large number of relevant primary authorities. Good legal researchers pause periodically in the research process to evaluate the usefulness of the research results. Secondary sources can aid you in this evaluation, by helping you narrow or broaden your focus. Thus, you may need to consult secondary sources at various points in your research process.

Secondary authorities can be powerful finding tools, but they cannot substitute for primary authority. Avoid citing secondary authority in a memo, brief, or other legal document unless there is no primary authority available to support a proposition. Despite the value of secondary sources, they are rarely cited in memoranda or briefs. Some sources, such as indexes for finding periodicals, are not "authority" at all. Rather, they are authority-finding tools and should never be cited. Encyclopedias, A.L.R. articles, and CLE material should be cited only as a last resort. Even sources that are secondary authority, including law review articles and treatises, should be cited infrequently. By citing secondary sources, you are admitting to your audience that you could not find any primary authority supporting your arguments, thereby weakening those arguments substantially.

Three exceptions exist. First, sometimes you need to summarize the development of the law. If no case has provided a summary, citing a treatise or law review article that traces that development could be helpful to your reader. Next, secondary authority may provide additional support for a point already cited to primary authority. For example, you can bolster an argument supported by a case, especially if it is from another jurisdiction, by also citing an article or treatise by a respected expert on the topic. Finally, as noted earlier, citation to secondary authority is appropriate when there is no law on point for an argument you are making. When dealing with new areas of the law or when arguing to expand or change the law, your only support may come from a law review article or other secondary authority.

Finally, secondary sources are not equally reliable. Carefully assess the quality and credibility of a given secondary source before relying on it either as a research tool or as persuasive authority for a legal analysis or argument. Moreover, do not cite to the primary authorities found in secondary sources without reading the primary authorities themselves. The secondary source might misstate the law or omit key information, or it might reference primary authority that is no longer valid.

II. Selecting the Most Relevant Secondary Sources

Secondary sources have different strengths and weaknesses and can be used in different ways while researching. You will be able to select the most useful secondary authorities for your research project if you first evaluate the strengths and weaknesses of a secondary source and the type of project you're working on. Spending focused time consulting one or two carefully selected secondary sources at the outset of a research project can save you valuable time and give you the necessary background knowledge to continue the research process.

Different research projects should also be tailored to use different secondary sources. For a broad overview of an area of law, an encyclopedia may be best. For in-depth analysis on a narrow topic, a law review article is more likely to be helpful. On cutting-edge issues, CLE material often covers new areas of law concisely. In litigation, court-approved forms and uniform jury instructions will be indispensable.

Consider your own background in the subject matter and the goals of your research, and select from these sources accordingly. How many secondary sources you use depends on the success of your early searches and the time available to you. It would almost never be prudent to check every source discussed in this chapter.

When determining which secondary source to research and how to use the information, you must decide the weight to give secondary authority in developing your own analysis. Consider the following criteria:

- *Who is the author?* The views of a respected scholar, an acknowledged expert, or a judge carry more weight than those of a student author or an anonymous editor.
- *When was the material published?* Especially for cutting-edge issues, a more recent article is likely to be more helpful. Even with more traditional issues, though, be sure that the material analyzes the current state of the law.
- *Where was the material published?* Traditional print sources almost always carry more weight than online websites.
- *Who was the publisher?* Articles published in established law journals are generally granted the most respect. A school's prestige and the length of the journal's existence influence how well established a journal is.
- *What depth is provided?* The more focused and thorough the analysis, the more useful the material will be.

- *How relevant is it to your argument?* If the author is arguing your exact point, the material will be more persuasive than if the author's arguments are only tangential to yours.
- *Has this secondary source been cited previously by courts?* If a court has found an article persuasive in the past, it is likely to find it persuasive again. Remember that the text of a secondary source may become primary authority if it is adopted by a court or legislature.

III. Researching in Print or Online

When researching in secondary sources, many researchers find that being able to quickly browse and view related content is important because it provides the context in which to understand information efficiently. Many researchers prefer print resources to online sources because of the ease of browsing to glean context. However, online vendors have steadily improved the presentation of secondary sources by including browsable tables of contents and other helpful features typically found in print.

Not all secondary sources are available online, and of those that are, some can be accessed only for a fee. Likewise, many law libraries have pared down their print resources to cut costs. Thus, on any given research project, you may need to consult both print and online sources to find relevant secondary authority.

Many researchers find that beginning with print sources is more effective than beginning in an online database. This is especially true when researching a complicated issue in an unfamiliar area of law. The process for researching secondary sources varies depending on the source. In general, though, whether you are researching in print or online, you will use a similar three-step process for most secondary sources. First, locate the relevant material in the main text, utilizing the index, a keyword search, or table of contents. Second, read the relevant material, taking notes on what you learn about your research question and what research leads you find. Third, update what you have found to make sure you are relying on the most current information for each source.

Many of the secondary sources discussed in this chapter can be found on Lexis, Westlaw, or other online services. The relevant databases can be searched by using terms-and-connectors or natural language searches in the full text, and by reviewing tables of contents. In the early phases of your research, beginning with the online table of contents is more likely to be effective than other approaches. After you gain background knowledge in an area of law, online full-text searches are more likely to be useful.

Table 4-1. Websites for Idaho Research

Website	Address	Secondary Sources and Links
Idaho State Bar	www.isb.idaho.gov	CLE materials; forms
Idaho State Judiciary	www.isc.idaho.gov	Court forms
Idaho State Law Library	www.isll.idaho.gov	Links to many websites under "Idaho Legal Resources"
State of Idaho Government	www.state.id.us/ government	Links to many Idaho resources under "Government"
University of Idaho College of Law Library	www.law.uidaho.edu	Links to many websites under "Idaho Resources"
Concordia University School of Law Library	www.law.cu-portland.edu/library	*Idaho Legal Information Sources Guide* included under "Research Guides"

Some secondary sources are available for free on state websites. A list of helpful websites for Idaho research is provided in Table 4-1. In addition, a quick search on Google may produce valuable leads. A law firm may refer to key statutes on its website, or an attorney may have posted a helpful summary of a legal issue.

IV. Treatises, Practice Guides, and Other Books

A book on a legal topic can provide an in-depth discussion of the topic and relevant references to primary authority. Legal texts include treatises, practice guides, hornbooks, and *Nutshells*. These books are arranged topically; all of these books share the purpose of covering a particular legal subject, such as contracts or civil procedure. They are distinguished mainly by their level of coverage.

Treatises are generally considered to be more comprehensive statements on a subject than hornbooks, which offer a slightly more summarized view. Practice guides typically cover an area of law thoroughly, but with a particular focus on the nuts and bolts of practice as opposed to the more theoretical approach of treatises or hornbooks. *Nutshells* are a series of books published by West that offer a very condensed explanation of law.

Accordingly, an attorney may use a treatise or practice guide to become familiar with a new area of law, while a law student might typically turn to a hornbook or *Nutshell* to prepare for class, or later to gain a better understanding of a class lecture. This chapter focuses on treatises and practice guides because they are more commonly used and cited than hornbooks and *Nutshells*.

Finding treatises, practice guides, and other books can be challenging. The best approach when researching an unfamiliar area of law is to ask someone who regularly researches or practices in the area. For example, in law school, ask a reference librarian or a faculty member. In a law firm, a librarian or an associate who researches in that area would be a good choice. You can also browse a library collection or use an online catalog in a larger library.

Some hornbooks and treatises are available online for a fee through services such as Bloomberg, Lexis, and Westlaw. Browsing the secondary sources databases of these online services should lead you to the individual databases for these hornbooks and treatises, even if you do not know the titles.

Once located, either in print or online, hornbooks and treatises are usually best approached using the index or table of contents to find the information needed. Many of the hornbooks and treatises that are available online include a browsable table of contents.

A. Treatises

Some treatises are so well known and widely respected that a colleague or supervisor may suggest that you begin research with a particular title. Examples include *Nimmer on Copyright*; Wright & Miller's *Federal Practice and Procedure*; and Moore's *Federal Practice*. The first example covers the law of copyright in one volume. The last two examples are multi-volume treatises.

Treatises are updated in print in a variety of ways. Bound volumes like Wright & Miller's *Federal Practice and Procedure* are updated with pocket parts — additional pages inserted in the back of a volume. Moore's *Federal Practice* is published in loose-leaf binders, which are updated by replacing outdated pages throughout the binder with current material. Each page is dated to show when it was last updated. Also, new pages at the beginning of loose-leaf binders are often in different colors to draw the reader's attention.

B. Idaho Practice Guides

The Idaho State Bar provides a number of publications on Idaho law. Topics are listed in on the bar's website. Each one covers one area of Idaho law in depth. The authors are typically practitioners with extensive experience in the legal area they are writing about, and the text is practice-oriented.

In addition to these bar books, West publishes the *Idaho Trial Practice Handbook 2d*, as well as a number of Idaho resources on Westlaw. More general practice guides are published by the Practising Law Institute (PLI), the American Law Institute (ALI), and the American Bar Association (ABA).

Practice guides published in loose-leaf binders are updated by replacing outdated pages. Some guides are published in hardbound volumes and updated with pocket parts. Still others are republished in full when they need to be updated. Always be sure that you are using the most current material available by checking the library catalog and browsing the shelves nearby.

C. Finding and Using Legal Books

Treatises, practice guides, hornbooks, and *Nutshells* can be located by using a library's catalog and searching for the general subject matter of a research project. For a well-known treatise, include the name of the author as one of the search terms. When searching for practice-oriented material, use the name of publisher (e.g., Idaho State Bar or American Law Institute). After finding one book on point, scan the other titles shelved around it for additional resources.

To use a treatise or other book, begin with either the table of contents or the index. In multi-volume treatises, the index is often in the last volume of the series. Locate your research terms and record the references given. A reference may be to a page number, section number, or paragraph number, depending on the publisher. The table of contents or index should indicate which type of number is referenced. Turn to that part of the book, read the text, and note any pertinent primary authority cited in the footnotes.

The authoritative value of a book depends largely on the reputation of the author. *Prosser & Keeton on the Law of Torts* is widely respected and cited by the courts. In contrast, a *Nutshell* on tort law is designed as a study guide for students or a quick overview for practitioners; it is not considered authoritative.

V. Legal Encyclopedias

Like other encyclopedias, legal encyclopedias provide general information on a wide variety of legal subjects. Legal encyclopedias are organized by subject matter under *topics*, which are presented alphabetically in bound volumes. The two national legal encyclopedias are *Corpus Juris Secundum* (C.J.S.) and *American Jurisprudence, Second Edition* (Am. Jur. 2d). C.J.S. is available on Westlaw; Am. Jur. 2d is available on both Lexis and Westlaw. Some larger states have their own encyclopedias, such as *California Jurisprudence* and *Florida Jurisprudence*. Idaho does not have its own encyclopedia.

To use an encyclopedia, review its softbound index volumes for your research terms. The references will include both an abbreviated word or phrase — the topic — and a section number.[1] The encyclopedia's topic abbreviations are explained in tables in the front of the index volumes. Select the bound volume containing a relevant topic. The spine of each volume includes the range of topics included in that volume.

Next, skim the material at the beginning of that topic for an overview and general information. Then turn to the particular section number given in the index and read the text there. The text of most encyclopedia entries is cursory because the goal of the writers is to summarize the law. Encyclopedia entries will identify significant variations that exist between different jurisdictions, but they do not attempt to resolve differences or recommend improvements in the law. Pocket parts sometimes provide updated commentary.

One potentially helpful feature of an encyclopedia is the list of footnotes accompanying the text. If a footnote refers to recent, primary authority from your jurisdiction, you will have made a great step forward in your research. However, because the footnotes in C.J.S. and Am. Jur. 2d cite to authorities from all American jurisdictions and tend to be dated, the chance of finding a reference to a recent, relevant case is limited. The encyclopedia's pocket parts may offer better prospects for researching primary authority.

An encyclopedia may also contain cross references to other sources. For example, C.J.S. includes cross references to relevant topics and key numbers in West's digests. Similarly, Am. Jur. 2d cross references *American Law Reports*, discussed later in this chapter.

VI. Legal Periodicals

A. Law Reviews and Journals

Law reviews and law journals publish scholarly articles written by law professors, judges, practitioners, and students. Each article explores in great detail a specific legal issue. Without the constraints of representing a client's interests

---

1. Do not confuse these topics and section numbers with the West digest system of topics and key numbers discussed in Chapter 11.

or deciding a particular case, an author is able to explore whether the laws currently in force are the best legal rules and to propose changes.

Reading articles published in law reviews and journals can provide a thorough understanding of current law because the authors often explain the existing law before making their recommendations. These articles may also identify weaknesses or new trends in the law that might address your client's situation. The many footnotes in law review and law journal articles can provide excellent summaries of relevant research. Although not as authoritative as articles written by recognized experts, student articles can provide clear and careful analysis and their footnotes are valuable research tools. Articles written by students are called "Notes" or "Comments."

Shorter law review pieces, generally written by students, simply summarize a recent case that the publication's editors consider important. These are called "Case Notes" or "Recent Developments." They notify readers of important developments in the law but do not analyze or critique the case in any depth. They are often not helpful beyond offering a short summary of the case and the court's analysis.

Law reviews and law journals are generally published by law students who were selected according to grades or through a competition for membership on the editorial board. Most law reviews have general audiences and cover a broad range of topics; examples include the *Concordia University Law Review* or *Idaho Law Review*. Many other law journals focus on a specific area of law, for example, the *Journal of Environmental Law and Litigation* and the *Columbia Journal of Transnational Law*. Still other law journals are "peer edited," meaning that law professors select and edit the articles to be published. Examples of this type of law journal are the *Journal of Legal Education* and the *Journal of the Association of Legal Writing Directors*.

Most periodicals are published first in soft-cover booklets, though some are published only online. Later, several issues may be bound into a single volume. Articles are located by volume number, the name of the journal, and the first page of the article.

Law review and law journal articles are not "updated" in the usual sense. You can, however, find out whether an article has been cited favorably or unfavorably by using a citator such as Shepard's on Lexis or KeyCite on Westlaw. Citators are covered in Chapter 12.

B. Bar Journals

Each state's bar journal contains articles of particular interest to attorneys practicing in that state. The Idaho State Bar publishes *The Advocate*. The American Bar Association publishes the *ABA Journal*, which has articles of general interest to attorneys across the nation.

Articles in bar journals are often shorter than articles published in law reviews and do not have the extensive footnotes found in law review articles. Moreover, the bar journal articles have a practitioner's focus.

C. Locating Articles

Periodical indexes offer the most accurate way of locating relevant articles. These indexes use specific subject headings into which various articles are classified. Though full-text searching is available on Lexis, Westlaw, and other services, for new researchers full-text searching is likely to produce an unwieldy number of articles, many of which are only tangentially related to your topic.

A popular index of legal periodicals is the *Current Law Index* (CLI). It is available in a database called LegalTrac, which is available in many law libraries. CLI is also available on Lexis and on Westlaw (called "Legal Resource Index"). The coverage of each version varies slightly, but all include articles at least back to 1980.

An important print index for legal periodicals is the *Index to Legal Periodicals and Books* (ILPB), previously called the *Index to Legal Periodicals*. This index is especially useful in finding older articles because its coverage extends back to the early 1900s. ILPB indexes articles by both subject and author in a single alphabetical list. Thus, articles under the subject heading "Education" may be followed by an article under the author heading "Edwards, Linda Holdeman." ILPB volumes are published yearly. They are not cumulative but are updated with soft-cover pamphlets. Monthly pamphlets are replaced by quarterly pamphlets. These quarterly pamphlets stay on library shelves until an annual bound volume becomes available, sometimes several years later. The ILPB is available online from Ebsco Discovery Service.[2] The Ebsco site contains indexes for non-legal periodicals, too.

---

2. The address is www.ebscohost.com/wilson.

HeinOnline offers full-text searching of a large number of journal articles. The search engine is not as sophisticated as those available on Lexis or Westlaw, but it can be effective. HeinOnline also includes the *Current Index to Legal Periodicals* (CILP) from Univ. of Washington Gallagher Law Library; it is published weekly.

One advantage to retrieving articles from HeinOnline is that the text is provided in PDF format, meaning that pagination looks exactly like the print copy (which makes citation of pinpoint pages easier) and footnotes accompany the relevant text (rather than being placed at the end of the article). Many law school libraries subscribe to HeinOnline, making it free to students and patrons.[3]

VII. *American Law Reports*

American Law Reports (A.L.R.) contains lengthy articles (formerly called annotations) and extensive research aids.[4] It is available on both Lexis and Westlaw.[5] The articles tend to focus on very narrow topics, take a practitioner's view, and provide a survey of the law in different jurisdictions. Thus, an article on the exact topic you're researching would be extremely helpful. The A.L.R. articles are written by lawyers who are knowledgeable but are not necessarily recognized experts.

A.L.R. has been published in several series over time. Early series contained both state and federal subjects. Currently, federal subjects are included in *A.L.R. Federal*, now in its second series. State subjects are discussed in numbered series: A.L.R.3d through A.L.R.6th. To locate an A.L.R. series in your library, search the library catalog for *American Law Reports*.

The most effective tool for locating annotations using A.L.R. in print is a *Quick Index*. One is available for the federal series; another is available for A.L.R.3d through A.L.R.6th. If you are not successful using a quick index, search the *A.L.R Index*, a multi-volume reference that covers the more recent numbered series and the federal series together. Another search tool is the *A.L.R. Digest*, which includes references to annotations, practice aids, and

---

3. The website is www.heinonline.org.
4. A.L.R. used to provide both annotations and full-length cases.
5. The complete set of A.L.R. is available on Westlaw. Lexis does not include the first series and includes only through A.L.R.6th in the state series and A.L.R. Fed 2d in the federal series.

A.L.R. cases. A.L.R. series are updated with pocket parts in print and are updated regularly on both Lexis and Westlaw. Also check the Annotation History Table in the index volumes to see whether an annotation has been supplemented or superseded by another annotation, rather than just updated in pocket parts.

VIII. Continuing Legal Education Publications

Attorneys in Idaho are required to attend continuing legal education (CLE) courses periodically to maintain their membership in the state's bar. These courses often present very practical information. Topics range from ethical issues in business law to building a personal-injury practice. Some CLE courses may be aimed at new lawyers just learning the fundamentals of practice; however, many CLE courses are intended to offer new insights on cutting-edge legal issues.

A CLE course may be led by a practitioner, judge, or law professor. Frequently, the person leading the course prepares handouts that include sample forms, sample documents, and explanations. These course materials are compiled by the bar association, bound, and published without being typeset. They are often available in law libraries; alternatively, the course materials (along with audio or video of the CLE course) may be purchased or rented from the bar. Check the Idaho State Bar's website under "Forms, Publications, and Other Resources."

Some of the largest publishers of similar materials are the Practising Law Institute (PLI), the American Law Institute (ALI), and the American Bar Association (ABA). CLE material is located by searching the library catalog by topic or by author, using the names of the more common CLE publishers as search terms.

CLE materials are sometimes published in loose-leaf binders, which are updated by replacing outdated pages. Others may be republished in full, or more recent CLE sessions may be held. Check the library catalog and browse the nearby shelves to be sure that the material you have is the most current that is available.

IX. Forms

Forms provide shortcuts in legal drafting. Especially when you are drafting a document for the first time in an unfamiliar area of law, a form provides an

Table 4-2. Sample Idaho Form

IN THE DISTRICT COURT OF THE _____ JUDICIAL DISTRICT
OF THE STATE OF IDAHO, IN AND FOR THE COUNTY OF _____

In the Matter of the termination)
of the parental rights of)
...................)
...................)

I (we), the undersigned, being the _____ of _____, do hereby give my (our) full and free consent to the complete and absolute termination of my (our) parental right(s), to the said _____, who was born _____, _____, unto _____, hereby relinquishing completely and forever, all legal rights, privileges, duties and obligations, including all rights of inheritance to and from the said _____, and I (we) do hereby expressly waive my (our) right(s) to hearing on the petition to terminate my (our) parental relationship with the said _____, and respectfully request the petition be granted.

DATED: ...., 20..
....

STATE OF IDAHO)
) ss.
COUNTY OF....)

On this ... day of ..., 20 ..., before me, the undersigned ..., ... (Judge or Magistrate) of the District Court of the ... Judicial District of the state of Idaho, in and for the county of ..., personally appeared 19 ..., known to me (or proved to me on the oath of ...) to be the person(s) whose name(s) is (are) subscribed to the within instrument, and acknowledged to me that he (she, they) executed the same.

IN WITNESS WHEREOF, I have hereunto set my hand and affixed my official seal the day and year in this certificate first above written.

....
(District Judge or Magistrate)

Source: Idaho Code § 16-2005, https://legislature.idaho.gov/statutesrules/idstat/Title16/T16CH20/SECT16-2005/.

excellent starting point by keeping you from reinventing the wheel.

Forms are available in a diverse range of sources. Idaho statutes provide forms for some particular situations. For example, I.C. § 16-2005 contains forms for consenting to the termination of the parent-child relationship. See Table 4-2. In a non-litigation context, I.C. § 32-401 contains language that must be included in a marriage license. To find statutory forms, search the

Idaho Code index or *West's Idaho Code Annotated* index both for the substantive content of the form and under the term "forms."

Many forms may also be found in court rules (discussed in Chapter 8), in practice guides (covered in Part VI of this chapter), and in CLE materials (discussed in Part VII of this chapter). A "formbook" may provide actual forms or suggested language that can be used in crafting your document. Examples of Idaho formbooks include *Idaho Probate and Estate Administration Forms* and *Idaho Real Estate Forms Book.* Federal forms are available in numerous titles, including *West's Federal Forms* and *American Jurisprudence Legal Forms 2d.* Search the library catalog by subject for topical formbooks.

The Idaho courts have provided a number of court-approved forms online.[6] The site has a variety of forms in the areas of family law, landlord-tenant matters, and domestic violence. In addition, the Idaho State Bar website provides links to forms under "Forms, Publications, and Other Resources."

Take care when using any form. Forms are designed for general audiences, not a particular client. Before using a form, be sure that you understand every word in the form and modify it to suit your client's needs. Do not simply fill in the blanks and assume that the form correctly represents your client's position. Unless a particular form is prescribed by statute or by a court, revise the wording to avoid unnecessary legalese.

X. Mini-Libraries and Loose-Leaf Services

A "mini-library" combines both primary and secondary sources under one title. In areas of law like taxation and environmental law, a single title may contain statutes, administrative regulations, annotations to cases and agency opinions, and commentary. The benefit is obvious: all of the material is gathered together so that the researcher does not have to consult multiple sources.

A. Print Resources

In print, a topical mini-library is often referred to as a loose-leaf service due to its pages being kept in loose-leaf, three-ring notebooks instead of being bound as books. While other secondary sources are also printed in this format, as discussed earlier in this chapter, the term "loose-leaf service" refers only to

---

6. The address is www.courtselfhelp.idaho.gov.

mini-libraries. Again, the loose-leaf format allows the publisher to send updates frequently and quickly; the outdated pages are removed and the new pages inserted on a regular basis. A loose-leaf service generally fills numerous volumes. The volumes may be arranged by topic, by statute, or by another system.

Loose-leaf services always have a "How to Use" section, which generally appears near the beginning of the first volume. Review this section before beginning research. Also consider skimming through a few volumes to become familiar with the organization of that particular service. Pay careful attention to each service's method and frequency of updating.

How you use a loose-leaf service depends on what you know at the beginning of a research project. In tax research, for example, to research a known section of the Internal Revenue Code, simply go to the *Standard Federal Tax Reporter* and find the volume whose spine indicates that the code section is included. In that volume, the statutory language will be followed by regulations issued by the Treasury Department, and then annotations. The first annotations will refer to cases decided by courts of general jurisdiction and the United States Tax Court; subsequent annotations will refer to rulings of the Internal Revenue Service. The treatment of that code section will conclude with commentary written by the publisher.

When you do not know the particular section of a loose-leaf that you need to research, begin with the topical index. Often this is the first or last volume of the series. Look up your research terms, and write down the reference numbers given. These will likely be paragraph numbers rather than page numbers. To maintain indexing despite frequent updates, loose-leaf services often are indexed by paragraph number. A "paragraph" may be just a few sentences, several actual paragraphs, or many pages in length. Even though the page numbers will change with future updates, the paragraph reference will remain constant.

Turn to each paragraph number referenced in the index under your key terms. Realize that the paragraph number may be for the statute, regulations, annotations, or commentary. Turn to previous and subsequent pages around that paragraph number to ensure that you have reviewed all relevant material.

B. Online Services

Loose-leaf services are available online; they are similar to the topical databases available on Lexis and Westlaw. Publishers such as Bureau of National Affairs (BNA) and Commerce Clearing House (CCH) gather loose-leaf type material together in one database and provide the advantage of full-text searching. For example, the *Standard Federal Tax Reporter* explained earlier is available

Table 4-3. Restatement Topics

Agency	Property, Mortgages
Conflicts of Law	Property, Servitudes
Contracts	Restitution
Foreign Relations Law	Suretyship and Guaranty
Judgments	Torts, Apportionment of Liability
Law Governing Lawyers	Torts, Products Liability
Property	Trusts
Property, Landlord Tenant	Unfair Competition
Property, Wills and Other Donative Transfers	

to subscribers in a database called CCH Tax Research Network. These sites sometimes add more explanations and tools than Lexis and Westlaw do, making them more user-friendly to novices.

Online databases often provide tutorials that are helpful introductions to the content and search techniques unique to each database. Some databases allow you to create a research trail that saves your query words and results. Printing these electronic trails will help you keep track of your research.

XI. Restatements

A restatement is an organized and detailed summary of the common law in a specific legal area. Restatements are available on both Lexis and Westlaw. While the *Restatement of Contracts* and the *Restatement of Torts* are the titles most familiar to general practitioners, other titles cover a broad range of topics. Table 4-3 shows Restatement topics.

Restatements result from collaborative efforts by committees of scholars, practitioners, and judges organized by the American Law Institute (ALI). These committees, led by a scholar called the *reporter*, draft text that explains the common law in rule format (i.e., they are written with outline headings similar to statutes, rather than in the narrative form of cases). The committees circulate the drafts for review and revision. The restatement that is published by ALI includes not only the text of the rules that embody the common law but also commentary, illustrations, and notes from the reporter.

Restatements were originally intended simply to restate the law as it existed, in an effort to build national consistency in key common-law areas. Over time, restatements grew more aggressive in stating what the authors thought the law should be.

A portion of a restatement becomes primary authority for a jurisdiction only if it is adopted by a court in a particular case. After a court has adopted a portion of a restatement, the committee's commentary and illustrations, as well as any notes provided by the reporter, may be valuable tools in interpreting the restatement. Cases in other jurisdictions that have adopted the restatement would be persuasive authority.

To find a relevant restatement, search the library catalog or online directory for the subject matter or search for *restatement*. When working with print volumes, use the table of contents, index, or appendix to find pertinent sections of a restatement. The text of each restatement section is followed by commentary and sometimes illustrations of key points made in the text. Appendix volumes list citations to cases that have referred to the restatement.

A restatement's language is updated only when a later version is published. However, the appendix volumes are updated with pocket parts and supplements, and online restatement databases are kept current. Shepardizing or KeyCiting a restatement section will reveal cases and articles that cite the restatement.

XII. Uniform Laws and Model Codes

Uniform laws and model codes are written by organizations that hope to harmonize the statutory laws of the fifty states. The most active of these organizations is the National Conference of Commissioners on Uniform State Laws (NCCUSL). Much of the work of writing uniform laws and model codes is done by experts who are law professors, judges, legislators, or attorneys.

Familiar examples of these secondary sources include the *Uniform Commercial Code* (UCC) and the *Model Penal Code*. Statutory language is drafted, then comments are solicited, and the language is finalized. The published uniform law or model code includes both the proposed statutory language and explanatory notes from the authors.

Generally, you would research a uniform law or model code only after one of its provisions had been enacted by your jurisdiction's legislature. At that point, the provision becomes primary authority and the explanatory notes become very persuasive secondary authority. Reviewing that commentary could help you understand a statute in your jurisdiction that was based on the uniform or model language. For example, every state has adopted a version of the UCC. In researching Idaho's commercial code, you could gain insights from commentary on the UCC that discussed the provisions adopted by Idaho. Additionally, the cases of other states that also adopted the same UCC provisions would be highly persuasive in interpreting Idaho's statute.

Uniform laws and model codes, along with official notes and explanations, are published by their authors. Additionally, commercial versions add commentary and often footnotes with case support. West publishes *Uniform Laws Annotated*, which offers indexing, text, and research annotations to uniform laws prepared under the direction of NCCUSL.

Finding a relevant uniform law or model code is similar to finding a restatement. Search the library catalog for the area of law, such as *criminal law* or *commercial transactions*; you may want to include in your search the words *model code* or *uniform law*. In the stacks, scan the titles nearby to determine whether more helpful commercial editions have been published. Within the volume or set of volumes containing the uniform law or model code, look in the table of contents, index, or appendix to locate relevant sections. Often they provide section-by-section indexing of the uniform or model provisions, similar to a digest entry.

XIII. Jury Instructions

At the close of a trial, the judge instructs the jury. These instructions outline the law; in other words, they tell lawyers preparing for trial what they have to prove in order to prevail. By examining the instructions in advance of trial, an attorney may better be able to present evidence to the jury. Even if a case ends before trial, knowing the instructions a jury would receive may produce more effective research.

The Idaho Supreme Court has not formally adopted a set of civil jury instructions, but a court-appointed Civil Instructions Jury Committee recommended such instructions to the Court. Criminal Jury Instructions have been adopted by the Court and recommended for use by the bench and bar. These instructions are both available on the Court's website under the "Jury Information" tab. The state law library also maintains copies of these jury instructions.

Chapter 5

Constitutions

A constitution is the highest legal authority in a jurisdiction. This chapter covers both the Idaho and the federal constitutions.

I. The Idaho Constitution

The Idaho Constitution was drafted in July and August of 1889 at a convention in the territorial capital of Boise City. It was ratified by the people of Idaho in November 1889, before the United States Congress had passed an enabling act. It was then approved by the United States Congress on July 3, 1890, and Idaho became a state. The Idaho Constitution has been amended 126 times, but it has served as the basic governing document for Idaho since its adoption. It has, despite the numerous amendments and one attempt at a wholesale revision,[1] never undergone a major revision. The Idaho Constitution remains in essentially the same form as when it was ratified in 1889, and many provisions have not changed since ratification.[2]

The Idaho Constitution has been called "the tie that binds, the single document whose task it is to hold Idaho together."[3] Indeed, many of its peculiarities and major features are a direct outgrowth of the geography of Idaho and the

---

1. During the late 1960s, the Idaho Constitutional Revision Commission met and studied the Idaho Constitution. Although charged with recommending revisions, it eventually proposed an entirely new constitution. However, after the Idaho Legislature approved the proposed constitution, the voters defeated it on the November 1970 ballot. For a brief history of the Idaho Constitutional Revision Commission, see www.lib.uidaho.edu/special-collections/Manuscripts/mg105.htm.
2. A complete list of the proposed and passed amendments to the Idaho Constitution can be found at https://sos.idaho.gov/elect/inits/index.html under the "Miscellaneous" heading.
3. Dennis C. Colson, *Idaho's Constitution: The Tie that Binds*, preface (U. of Idaho Press 1991).

historical circumstances under which it was drafted.[4] For instance, the Idaho Constitution is the only state constitution to deal with water rights; the most recent amendment guarantees the right to hunt, fish, and trap. Like many state constitutions, the Idaho Constitution is long, detailed, and specific.

Nevertheless, provisions of the Idaho Constitution parallel many of the most familiar provisions of the United States Constitution. Article I of the Idaho Constitution guarantees the right of eminent domain, the right to free speech, the right to a jury trial, the right to keep and bear arms, freedom of religion, and freedom of assembly. Articles III through V provide for legislative, executive, and judicial departments of the state government. Table 5-1 lists the articles of the Idaho Constitution.

A. Researching the Idaho Constitution

1. Locating Constitutional Provisions

Because of the numerous issues covered by the Idaho Constitution, begin by checking to see whether a constitutional provision affects your client's interests in any new project. As explained in Chapter 1, research begins with generating a list of research terms from the facts and issues of the client's problem. Next, chose which sources to use and your research strategies as described in Chapters 2 and 3.

The full text of the Idaho Constitution is available on the legislature's website, and this site provides a keyword search function.[5] The major commercial providers of legal documents, Lexis and Westlaw, both contain databases with the Idaho Constitution. Searching a table of contents on one of these sites may be more efficient than constructing full-text searches of the entire constitution, especially when searching for general terms. Likewise, Casemaker allows you to search using the table of contents and the text, as do some other free and commercial providers. Both print compilations of the Idaho Code also reprint the Idaho Constitution in their first volumes and provide references to the Idaho Constitution in the index.

2. Interpreting the Idaho Constitution

In Idaho, "[t]he fundamental object in construing constitutional provisions is to ascertain the intent of the drafters by reading the words as written, em-

---

4. *See id.*; *see also* Donald Crowley & Florence Heffron, *The Idaho State Constitution: A Reference Guide*, 1 (G. Alan Tarr ed., Greenwood Press 1994).

5. The website is legislature.idaho.gov/statutesrules/idconst/.

Table 5-1. Articles of the Constitution of Idaho

Article I	Declaration of Rights
Article II	Distribution of Powers
Article III	Legislative Department
Article IV	Executive Department
Article V	Judicial Department
Article VI	Suffrage and Elections
Article VII	Finance and Revenue
Article VIII	Public Indebtedness and Subsidies
Article IX	Education and School Lands
Article X	Public Institutions
Article XI	Corporations, Public and Private
Article XII	Corporations, Municipal
Article XIII	Immigration and Labor
Article XIV	Militia
Article XV	Water Rights
Article XVI	Livestock
Article XVII	State Boundaries
Article XVIII	County Organization
Article XIX	Apportionment
Article XX	Amendments
Article XXI	Schedule and Ordinance

ploying their natural and ordinary meaning, and construing them to fulfill the intent of the drafters."[6] In order to do so, Idaho courts apply the general rules of statutory construction to provisions of the Idaho Constitution.[7] The rules of statutory construction apply both to original provisions and to amendments to the Idaho Constitution.[8]

When a constitutional provision is plain, clear, and unambiguous, the courts must give the provision the meaning its wording clearly implies.[9] Idaho courts engage in constitutional interpretation only if a provision is ambiguous. The

---

6. *Sweeney v. Otter*, 119 Idaho 135, 139, 804 P.2d 308, 312 (1990).
7. *Id.* at 138, 804 P.2d at 311.
8. *Id.*
9. *Westerberg v. Andrus*, 114 Idaho 401, 403, 757 P.2d 664, 666 (1988).

court's interpretation should determine the meaning of the language used in light of conditions as they existed at the time the provision was adopted.[10] For original provisions, Idaho courts presume that the words used in a constitution have the "natural and popular meaning in which they are usually understood by the people who adopted them."[11] For these provisions, the debates from the 1889 Idaho Constitutional Convention are the most convincing evidence as to what the members of that convention intended when they drafted the constitution.[12] For amendments, Idaho courts presume that the legislature and the people who voted on the amendment understood the state of the law before the amendment.[13]

3. Researching Related Cases

Even when the language of a constitutional provision is clear, the next step after locating a relevant constitutional provision is to read cases that discuss the constitutional provision to understand how the Idaho courts have applied it to various factual situations. Both the major commercial providers and both print compilations of the Idaho Code provide an efficient way to research these cases through their editorial enhancements. Thus, even if you locate a relevant constitutional provision using a different resource, you should turn to Lexis, Westlaw, or a print version of the Idaho Code for this step in researching the Idaho Constitution.

In any of these resources, locate the relevant provision, then review the annotations that follow. This process mirrors the process for finding cases that interpret and apply statutes and is discussed in more detail in Chapter 6. Alternately, you can find cases that interpret and apply the Constitution using the methods for finding judicial opinions discussed in more detail in Chapter 11.

4. Researching the Constitution's History

In addition to researching case law, you should also research the history of the constitutional provision. This history can help you better understand the context of the provision and apply it to your client's situation. It can also aid you in convincing a court how the provision should be interpreted.

---

10. *Toncray v. Budge*, 14 Idaho 621, 647, 95 P. 26, 34–35 (1908).
11. *Taylor v. State*, 62 Idaho 212, 217, 109 P.2d 879, 880 (1941).
12. *Fralick v. Guyer*, 36 Idaho 648, 653, 213 P. 337, 338 (1923); *Idaho Tel. Co. v. Baird*, 91 Idaho 425, 429, 423 P.2d 337, 341 (1967).
13. *Poss v. Meeker Mach. Shop*, 109 Idaho 920, 928, 712 P.2d 621, 629 (1985).

Table 5-2. Collateral References

§ 5. Right of Habeas Corpus. — The privilege of the writ of habeas corpus shall not be suspended, unless in case of rebellion or invasion, the public safety requires it, and then only in such a manner as shall be prescribed by law.

***

Collateral References. Discussion of this section in constitutional convention. Constitutional Convention Proceedings, Vol. I, p. 146; Vol. II, p. 1589.

Source: *Idaho Code*, Constitution of the State of Idaho, pages 60–61.

Fortunately, the constitutional drafters employed stenographers to make a verbatim record of the proceedings of the constitutional convention. In 1911, these records were transcribed and published in two volumes: *Proceedings and Debates of the Constitutional Convention of Idaho, 1889*. To find the debates covering the provision you are researching, refer to the "Collateral Reference" annotations following the constitutional provision on Lexis or in *Idaho Code*. There you will find the volume and page number where the debates on that provision are found in the *Proceedings and Debates of the Constitutional Convention of Idaho, 1889*. You may then easily locate the relevant portions of the debates. Table 5-2 provides an example of these annotations.

If you do not have access to Lexis or *Idaho Code*, you may find the relevant portions of the debates by using *Proceedings and Debates of the Constitutional Convention of Idaho, 1889*. Volume II contains an "Index to Articles and Sections." This index lists the articles and sections of the Idaho Constitution and provides page numbers where the debates on those provisions are found. A digital version of these volumes is available on the legislature's website.[14]

Since all amendments to the Idaho Constitution originate in the Idaho Legislature and are then voted on by the people of Idaho,[15] the process of researching constitutional amendments parallels that of researching legislative history discussed in Chapter 7. For amendments or provisions of the Constitution added after the convention, the research process begins by locating the bill number that proposed the constitutional amendment. On Lexis the bill number is under "Compiler's Notes"; on Westlaw it is under "Credits." Table 5-3 provides an example of "Compiler's notes."

With the bill number, you can locate information produced by the legislature regarding the amendment. The information available varies depending on the

---

14. The address is legislature.idaho.gov/statutesrules/idconst/.
15. Idaho Const. art. XX, §§ 1–4.

Table 5-3. Compiler's Notes for Article I, § 7

Compiler's notes. As originally adopted, this section provided as follows:

"**§ 7. Right to trial by jury.** — The right of trial by jury shall remain inviolate; but in civil actions, three-fourths of the jury may render a verdict, and the legislature may provide that in all cases of misdemeanors five-sixths of the jury may render a verdict. A trial by jury may be waived in all criminal cases not amounting to felony, by the consent of both parties, expressed in open court, and in civil actions by the consent of the parties, signified in such manner as may be prescribed by law. In civil actions and cases of misdemeanor the jury may consist of twelve or of any number less than twelve upon which the parties may agree in open court."

It was amended as proposed by S.L. 1933, p. 468, S.J.R. No. 1, and ratified at the general election in November 1934, to read as follows:

***

It was further amended, as proposed by S.L. 1982, p. 931, S.J.R. No. 112 and ratified at the general election on November 2, 1982 to read as it now appears.

Source: *Idaho Code*, Constitution of the State of Idaho, page 66 (emphasis added).

year the bill was introduced. However, for more recent constitutional amendments, you may be able to compile a *statement of purpose* and *fiscal note*, a *procedural history*, and *committee minutes* relating to the bill. Follow the process for compiling a legislative history discussed in Chapter 7.

In addition to the information produced by the legislature, also check to see what information was provided to the voters. Beginning with the year 1949, voters were provided with a *Statement of Meaning and Purpose and Effect of Adoption*.[16] For recent years, from 1998 to present, these materials are available online through the Secretary of State's website.[17] Both the Legislative Services Office[18] and the Elections Division of the Secretary of State's Office[19] have copies of older information, although their collections may be incomplete.

---

16. Beginning in 1949, the Attorney General provided these. Beginning in 1976, they were provided by the Legislative Council. Beginning in 2010, the name was changed to *Statement of Meaning and Purpose and Result to be Accomplished*.

17. The address is sos.idaho.gov/elect/inits/index.html

18. The Legislative Services Office is located in the north end of the basement of the Capitol building in Boise. Contact information is available on its website at www.legislature.idaho.gov.

19. The Secretary of State's administrative office is located on the second floor of the east wing of the Capitol building in Boise. The Commercial Office is located at 450 N. 4th St., Boise, Idaho 83702. The mailing address for both is P.O. Box 83720, Boise, Idaho 83720-0080. The phone number is (208) 334-2300.

II. Locating and Researching the United States Constitution

Just as the Idaho Constitution is the foundational document of Idaho, the federal constitution provides the foundation for the law of the United States. Both Lexis and Westlaw provide databases containing the federal constitution, as well as editorial features designed to help the researcher locate relevant case law and secondary opinions. The text is also available for free at both state and federal websites.[20] Likewise, print versions of the United States Code and the Idaho Code contain the text of the federal constitution and editorial enhancements to aid the researcher.

---

20. Govinfo.gov provides access to an online edition of the *Constitution of the United States of America: Analysis and Interpretation*. This annotated constitution is a great starting point for researching the federal constitution.

Chapter 6

Statutes

A statute is written law, enacted by the legislative branch. In the hierarchy of legal authority, statutes come just below constitutions and before regulations and judicial opinions. Because of their importance, almost every research project should include statutory research to determine if a statute is relevant to the problem.

Frequently, a statute will define a client's rights or responsibilities. A statute may set penalties for failure to comply with a statutory mandate. Some statutes address new issues that were not dealt with at common law; for example, regulation of cryptocurrency is a relatively new statutory area. Other statutes may codify or alter the common law, for example, consolidating embezzlement, extortion, false pretenses, cheats, misrepresentations, larceny, and receiving stolen goods into a single offense known as theft. Some statutes are driven by policy concerns. For instance, in Idaho, school teachers have a duty to warn of a student's suicidal tendencies only if they have direct evidence of those tendencies. Even if no statute affects the substance of a claim, a statute of limitations may prescribe the period during which the claim may be brought.

This chapter explains how to find and analyze Idaho state statutes. Research into other state statutes and federal statutes is also covered briefly.

I. Idaho Statutory Research

A. Structure of Idaho Statutes

After the legislature enacts bills, they are codified as statutes. Codification is the process in which laws enacted by the legislature are grouped according to subject matter. The codified statutes in Idaho are called the Idaho Code. In Idaho, statutory law is codified under the supervision of the Idaho Code Com-

Table 6-1. Chapters in Title 32, Domestic Relations

1. Persons
2. Marriage — Nature and Validity of Marriage Contract
3. Solemnization of Marriage
4. Marriage Licenses, Certificates, and Records
5. Annulment of Marriage
6. Divorce — Grounds and Defenses
7. Divorce Actions
8. Divorces for Insanity
9. Husband and Wife — Separate and Community Property
10. Parent and Child
11. Uniform Child Custody Jurisdiction and Enforcement Act
12. Mandatory Income Withholding for Child Support
13. Parent Responsibility Act
14. Coordinated Family Services
16. Financial Institution Data Match Process
17. De Facto Custodian Act

Source: https://legislature.idaho.gov/statutesrules/idstat/Title32/. Note that Chapter 15 has been reserved.

mission.[1] The official compilation of statutes is *Idaho Code* (I.C.), published by Michie.

The Idaho Code is divided into seventy-four *titles*, each on a broad subject, such as Alcoholic Beverages, Law Libraries, Public Lands, and Worker's Compensations. Within each title, statutes are grouped into *chapters* on more narrow topics. Table 6-1 is an example of chapters under Title 32, Domestic Relations. Each statute in a title and chapter is assigned a specific number. In citations to Idaho statutes, the title, chapter, and statutory number are used. In the example "I.C. § 73-201," the statute is located in Title 73, Chapter 2, and has been assigned the specific number 01.

B. Researching the Idaho Code

The first step in statutory research is to find and read any relevant statutes. If you already know the citation for a relevant statute, you can easily find it

---

1. I.C. §§ 73-201–73-221.

Table 6-2. Outline for Idaho Statutory Research

1. Search online by entering the citation, reviewing the table of contents, skimming an online index, or conducting a full-text search. Alternatively, in print pull the correct title if you know the citation or look up research terms in the index of *Idaho Code* (I.C.) or *West's Idaho Code Annotated* (W.I.C.A.) to find references to relevant statutes.
2. Read, and analyze statutes.
3. Read the annotations after the statute to find citations to cases that interpret or apply the statute.
4. Read and analyze the relevant cases.

for free on the legislature's website[2] or by pulling the correct Title from a print version. If you don't know the citation, you should generate research terms and then determine which source you want to search and determine a research strategy to follow to find any relevant statutes. Once you've found all the relevant statutes, you should read and analyze the statutes and then use annotations to find and read any relevant cases that interpret or apply the statute. Table 6-2 outlines the steps in the statutory research process. Overall, the process for researching the Idaho Code is remarkably similar using either online services or print resources.

C. Researching the Idaho Code Online

1. Find by Citation

You can enter the citation for the statute into the main search box on Lexis, Westlaw, Casemaker, and other commercial services. While not quite as simple, you can locate the text of statutes on the legislature's website. Click on the "Laws and Rules" and then "Idaho Statutes" from the resulting menu; scroll to the bottom of the screen and click on the "Search the Idaho Statutes and Constitution" link. You can then enter a citation or keywords to find the relevant statute.

2. Tables of Contents Searching

Many commercial services allow you to search for Idaho Statutes by accessing the table of contents for the Idaho Code. On Lexis, choose "Idaho" as the jurisdiction from "State" content, then select "Idaho Code Annotated." From

---

2. The address is legislature.idaho.gov/statutesrules/idstat/.

Table 6-3. Using Search Terms on Westlaw and Lexis

Westlaw	Lexis
1. Click on "State Materials" below the main search bar.	1. Click on "State Materials" below the main search bar.
2. Choose "Idaho."	2. Choose "Idaho."
3. Click on "Idaho Statutes & Court Rules."	3. Click on "ID-Idaho Code Annotated."
4. Enter search terms.	4. Enter a natural language search in the search box or use "Terms" boxes to construct a terms-and-connectors search.
5. Narrow results by applying filters in the left margin: search within results, effective date, or statute title.	
6. Read the resulting statutes.	5. Narrow results by entering further searched in the "Search within results" box on the left margin.
	6. Read the resulting statutes.

there, expand the various codes until you find a Title that might contain relevant statutory provisions. You can then expand the individual titles to look at chapters and sections. On Westlaw, choose "Idaho" as the jurisdiction under "State Materials," then select "Idaho Statutes & Court Rules." You can then expand the titles and sections to review individual statutes. On Casemaker, select "Idaho" as your jurisdiction, and then select "Statutes." You can expand the titles to review the sections and read individual statutes.

From the legislature's website select "Laws and Rules" and then "Idaho Statutes" from the resulting menu. You can select any title and resulting chapter to find a list of the statutes in that chapter. Click on the section number and that section will be displayed.

3. Researching with Search Terms

Both Lexis and Westlaw allow you to search for statutes using natural language or terms-and-connectors searches. The best approach to finding Idaho statutes, however, is to begin with a narrow search. On either database, select Idaho as the jurisdiction and then select the database for Idaho Statutes. From the resulting screen, enter your search, then narrow the results using segments or fields. Table 6-3 details this approach for both services.

The legislature's website allows you to conduct an advanced search. First, click on the "Laws and Rules" and then "Idaho Statutes" from the resulting menu; scroll to the bottom of the screen and click on the "Search the Idaho

Statutes and Constitution" link. You can then enter a citation or keywords to find the relevant statute. If this doesn't produce useful results, the top menu bar provides options for "Menu-assisted," "Advanced," "Natural Language," and "Preferences"; some of these options are more useful than others.

4. Index Searching

Westlaw allows researchers to search the Idaho Code by an index feature. This allows you to search for relevant statutes by topic. Because statutes use broad, general language searching an index can be more efficient than conducting a terms-and-connectors search; index searching also limits the search to the text of the statute itself. To access the index, choose "Idaho" as your jurisdiction under "State Materials." Next, select "Idaho Statutes & Court Rules." You will see a link for "Idaho Statutes Index" in the list on the right side of the screen. You can browse the index or enter your search terms in the resulting screen.

D. Researching Idaho Statutes in Print

Idaho Code (I.C.) and *West's Idaho Code Annotated* (W.I.C.A) are the two annotated compilations of the Idaho Code. Both I.C. and W.I.C.A. are compiled using the same classification and numbering system explained above. The spine of each volume of I.C. and W.I.C.A. indicates which titles are contained in that particular volume. How you begin to research Idaho statutes depends on the information you have when you begin your work.

1. Finding by Citation

Sometimes, you will be told exactly which statute controls your client's situation. Your supervisor may know from experience that I.C. § 32-922 deals with the formalities of a premarital agreement. In that case, review the spine of either I.C. or W.I.C.A. to find the volume containing Title 32; then look through the volume numerically to find the chapter and statute. In both I.C. and W.I.C.A., the statute numbers are included on the top, outside corner of each page.

2. Searching the Index for Research Terms

Take the list of research terms you developed using a technique described in Chapter 2 to the two, soft-bound index volumes shelved at the end of I.C. or W.I.C.A. These volumes are published annually to address all legislation through the most recent session of the legislature. Search for every one of your research terms. As you find terms in the index volumes, write down any statutory references given. Do not stop reviewing the index after finding just one statutory reference; several statutes may address your issue. Note that "*et seq.*" refers to the statute listed and the sections that follow it. Sometimes a research term will be included in the index but will be followed by a cross reference to another index term. Referring to that term may lead you to relevant statutes.

Then, for each statutory citation you found in the index, select the volume of I.C. or W.I.C.A. that contains the title of the statute, and then find the chapter and the statute itself. Because the publishers do not print new volumes of these compilations after the legislature meets each year, the most current statutory text may appear in a pocket part. Always check both the main volume and the pocket part to determine the current statutory language.[3]

E. Reading Statutes

This is the most important step in the statutory research process: *Read* the statute very carefully. Too many researchers fail to take the time necessary to read the language of the statute and consider all its implications before deciding whether it is relevant to the research problem. Statutes are the product of many people negotiating and compromising, so their wording is infrequently clear enough to convey every possible meaning on a quick skim or on one reading. Thus, careful research may require you to read a statute several times before you understand its meaning and relevance.

Additionally, to understand a single statute, you may have to read other, related statutes. One statute may contain general provisions while another contains definitions. Yet another statute may contain exceptions to the general rule. In the example in Table 6-4, the statute refers to recording "under the provisions of this chapter," indicating that other statutes in the same chapter should be read to fully understand the meaning of this statute.

To guarantee that you understand a statute, break it into elements. Using bullet points or an outline format is helpful for identifying key ideas. Connecting words and punctuation provide guidance for the relationships between different requirements of the statute. Small words like "and" and "or" can drastically change the meaning of a statute. With "and" all statutory require-

---

3. Also note that your client's situation may be governed by statutory language as it appeared at the time of the facts giving rise to your client's case. In order to determine the exact language of the statute, it is necessary to consult the *Idaho Session Laws*. This process is explained in Chapter 7.

Table 6-4. Example Idaho Statute

32-918 Marriage settlements — Record.

(1) When such contract is acknowledged or proved, it must be recorded in the office of the recorder of every county in which any real estate may be situated which is granted or affected by such contract.

(2) (a) A summary of the contract may be recorded in lieu of the contract, *under this chapter or the laws of this state*, if the requirements of this section are substantially met.

(b) A summary of the contract shall be signed and acknowledged by all parties to the original contract. The summary of the contract shall clearly state:

- (i) The names of the parties to the original contract;
- (ii) The complete mailing address of all parties;
- (iii) The title and date of the contract;
- (iv) A description of the interest or interests in real property created by the contract; and
- (v) The legal description of the property.

(c) Other elements of the contract may be stated in the summary.

(3) If the requirements of this section are met, the summary of the contract may be *recorded under the provisions of this chapter* and, as to the contents of the summary only, it shall have the same force and effect as if the original contract had been recorded, and constructive notice shall be deemed to be given concerning the contents of the summary and the existence of the contract to any subsequent purchasers, mortgagees, or other persons or entities that acquire an interest in the real property.

Source: https://legislature.idaho.gov/statutesrules/idstat/Title32/T32CH9/SECT32-918/ (emphasis added).

ments must be present for the statute to apply, while with "or" only one part is needed. Also, note the difference between "must" and "shall," which mandate action, and "may," which permits action. In Table 6-5, I.C. § 32-918 is broken into elements.

F. Using Annotations: Finding Cases That Interpret or Apply Statutes

It is rare to locate a relevant statute and then immediately apply it to your client's situation without first having to research case law. Legislatures write statutes generally to apply to a wide array of circumstances. In order to predict how a court may apply a statute to your client's situation, you must learn how courts have interpreted the statute and applied it in the past.

Table 6-5. Requirements for Recording a Marriage Settlement

- acknowledged or proved contract *must* be recorded in county of real estate affected by contract

  or
- summary of contract *may* be recorded
  - summary *must* be signed and acknowledged by parties to original contract, *and*
  - summary *must* contain *all*:
    - names of parties to original contract
    - mailing address of parties
    - title and date of contract
    - description of interest created by contract
    - legal description of real property
  - other elements of contract *may* be summarized
- if provisions met, recording of summary gives constructive notice

Publishers have recognized the need to find cases that apply or interpret statutes as well as the statutory language itself. Some, therefore, connect these two legal sources by including *annotations* to case law with the statutory text. Annotations are short summaries of the cases that have applied or interpreted the statute. Because not all publishers or services provide annotations, using an annotated code to conduct research can be much more powerful and efficient than using an unannotated code.

Each summary includes the name of the case and a citation to the case. The citation indicates which court decided that case and where the case can be found. You must record the citation information accurately in order to find the case in the reporters or online.

Both Lexis and Westlaw follow the statutory language with annotations. On Lexis the list of annotations is available after the statutory text under "Annotations" and then "Case Notes"; on Westlaw the list of annotations is available under the "Notes of Decisions" tab near the top of the screen. On both services these are organized topically. You can click on the various topics with in the list of annotations to review cases related to that topic.

Following the text of each statute in I.C. and W.I.C.A. are short summaries of cases that interpret or apply that statute; in I.C. these appear under the heading "Judicial Decisions," and in W.I.C.A. they appear under the heading

"Notes of Decisions."[4] Both Idaho and federal cases appear. In both statutory compilations, when the statute has a large number of annotations, they are organized into a topical outline to help the researcher quickly find the sections containing the cases most on point. In I.C. the cases are listed in chronological order; they appear in reverse chronological order in W.I.C.A. If courts have interpreted or applied that statute since the volume was published, summaries of those cases will appear in the pocket part.

II. Applying and Interpreting Idaho Statutes

Most often, applying a statute means reading the words carefully, referring to related statutes, analyzing cases that apply those statutes, and applying the law to the facts of your client's situation.

In litigation, the role of an Idaho court in construing a statute is to determine the intent of the legislature in enacting the statute.[5] In order to do this, the court engages in a two-tiered analysis. The court begins by reading the statute and then other statutes in that title to determine if the meaning is clear.[6] The court will also look to cases that have interpreted that statutory section or other sections within the same title. During this stage in the analysis, the court "will not deal in any subtle refinements of the legislation, but will ascertain and give effect to the purpose and intent of the legislature, based on the whole act and every word therein, lending substance and meaning to the provisions."[7] At this level, words are given their plain and ordinary meaning, and construed according to context; however, technical words or phrases, words that "have acquired a peculiar and appropriate meaning in law," or words that are defined in other statutes are construed "according to such peculiar and appropriate meaning or definition."[8] If, after this stage in the analysis the language of a statute is clear and unambiguous, statutory construction is unnecessary, and

---

4. I.C. also contains *decisions under prior law*, explaining cases that are no longer relevant under the new statutory language.

5. I.C. § 73-102; *Ada Co. Bd. of Equalization v. Highlands, Inc.*, 141 Idaho 202, 208, 108 P.3d 349, 355 (2005).

6. I.C. § 73-113; *see also Williamson v. City of McCall*, 135 Idaho 452, 455, 19 P.3d 766, 769 (2001) ("The interpretation should begin with an examination of the literal words of the statute, and this language should be given its plain, obvious, and rational meaning.").

7. *Ada Co. Assessor v. Roman Catholic Diocese of Boise*, 123 Idaho 425, 428, 849 P.2d 98, 101 (1993).

8. I.C. § 73-113.

the court need only determine the application of the words to the facts of the case at hand.[9]

The court moves to the second tier of analysis only if a statute is ambiguous. A statute is ambiguous when the language is capable of more than one reasonable construction.[10] However, "[a]mbiguity is not established merely because differing interpretations are presented to a court; otherwise, all statutes subject to litigation would be considered ambiguous."[11] To determine the intent of the legislature when examining an ambiguous statute, the court examines "not only the literal words of the statute, but also the reasonableness of proposed constructions, the public policy behind the statute, and its legislative history."[12] The legislative history of a statute includes deliberations of the House and Senate, as well as any committees that considered the bill that was enacted as this statute. Chapter 7 explains how to conduct legislative history research. When examining the reasonableness of proposed constructions, the court may follow maxims of statutory construction.[13]

III. Researching the Statutes of Other States

The same basic research process applies to statutory research in other states, but with some important differences. Some states' statutes are like Idaho's in containing a title, a chapter, and a section number. This is true for Wyoming, although it contains three numerals, e.g., Wyo. Stat. Ann. § 20-1-201. In contrast, other states, such as Oregon, Washington, and Nevada contain just the chapter and statute number. For instance, the Oregon statute defining second-degree burglary is located in Or. Rev. Stat. § 164.215, where 164 is the chapter and 215 is the statutory number. California combines numbers with code names, producing statutory citations such as Cal. Civ. Pro. Code § 340.1.

---

9. *Hamilton v. Reeder Flying Serv.*, 135 Idaho 568, 571, 21 P.3d 890, 893 (2001).

10. *Porter v. Bd. of Trustees, Preston Sch. Dist. No. 201*, 141 Idaho 11, 13, 105 P.3d 671, 673 (2004); *State v. Schwartz*, 139 Idaho 360, 362, 79 P.3d 719, 721 (2003); *Jen-Rath Co., Inc. v. Kit Mfg. Co.*, 137 Idaho 330, 335, 48 P.3d 659, 664 (2002).

11. *Hamilton*, 135 Idaho at 572, 21 P.3d at 894.

12. *Hayden Lake Fire Protec. Dist. v. Alcorn*, 141 Idaho 388, 398–99, 111 P.3d 73, 83–84 (2005) (quoting *Schwartz*, 139 Idaho at 362, 79 P.3d at 721); *Gillihan v. Gump*, 140 Idaho 264, 266, 92 P.3d 514, 516 (2004).

13. An invaluable tool in statutory construction is *Statutes and Statutory Construction* by Norman J. Singer, commonly referred to as *Sutherland Statutory Construction*. For an excellent summary of the numerous canons of statutory construction, refer to Karl N. Llewellyn, *Remarks on the Theory of Appellate Decision and the Rules or Canons About How Statutes Are to Be Construed*, 3 Vand. L. Rev. 395 (1950).

State codes are widely available online. Gateway sites like FindLaw and the Cornell site provide links to reliable sources. Lexis and Westlaw both provide annotated versions of state codes.

IV. Federal Statutes

The United States Code is widely available online. The Office of the Law Revision Counsel of the House of Representatives provides a searchable code.[14] The Cornell Legal Information Institute also provides the code and searching capacity.[15] Federal statutes are also available on Casemaker, Lexis, Westlaw, and other commercial sources.

The official text of federal statutes is published in the *United States Code* (U.S.C.). Federal statutes are codified in U.S.C. under fifty-four titles. Within each title, individual statutes are assigned section numbers. To cite a federal statute, include both the title and the section number. The federal statute granting appellate jurisdiction to federal appellate courts is 28 U.S.C. § 1291 (2012). Title 28 is devoted to courts and judicial matters, and 1291 is the section number assigned to this statute. The date of publication of that volume of U.S.C. was 2012.

U.S.C. is updated infrequently and does not include annotations, so it is of limited value in research. The more commonly used print sources are *United States Code Annotated* (U.S.C.A.) and *United States Code Service* (U.S.C.S.). Both U.S.C.A. and U.S.C.S. contain the text of federal statutes and references to related research sources, including annotations to cases interpreting or applying each federal statute. If the current text of the statute is not yet available in U.S.C., citing U.S.C.A. or U.S.C.S. is preferred over citing an online source. Even if you use Lexis, Westlaw, or another online source to find a federal statute, cite it to one of the print codifications listed above.

---

14. This is available at http://uscode.house.gov.
15. The address is at www.law.cornell.edu/uscode.

Chapter 7

Bill Tracking and Legislative History

This chapter covers the process by which the Idaho State Legislature enacts laws. It begins with an overview of the process by which the statutory laws of Idaho are enacted and amended. The chapter then describes the process of *bill tracking*, monitoring the status of a current bill that may or may not ultimately be enacted. Lawyers track bills that may affect a client's interest when they are acting in an advisory role. The chapter then explains how to research the *legislative history* of a statute that has already been enacted. Legislative history research is most often relevant in litigation when a lawyer is trying to convince a court to interpret an ambiguous statute in a way that is favorable to a client's position. Understanding the legislative process is important here because that process produces documents that may help determine the legislature's intent in passing a statute, which is key to statutory interpretation.

To end the discussion of Idaho legislation, this chapter covers the initiative and referendum processes. Next, opinions of the Idaho Attorney General are considered because they can be important in interpreting legislation. The chapter then concludes with an overview of federal bill tracking and legislative history.

I. The Legislative Process

The Idaho State Legislature consists of a Senate, with thirty-five members, and a House of Representatives, with seventy members. The legislature meets for regular sessions every year.[1] The general process of enacting or changing

---

1. Prior to 1969, the Idaho State Legislature met biennially in odd-numbered years. *Idaho Blue Book*, 123 (18th ed., Secretary of State Ben Ysursa 2005–2006). Each legislature now has two yearly sessions; the First Regular Session convenes the January after elections and the Second Regular Session convenes the following January. Ctr. for Pub. Policy & Admin., *Idaho Legislative Manual*, 5 (Boise State University 1998).

laws in Idaho is similar to that of the United States Congress and other states. The legislature does not create a detailed record of its proceedings as bills move through the legislative process, but the following summary notes documents produced during the legislative process in Idaho.

The genesis of a *bill* begins with an idea for legislation by a citizen, interest group, state agency, or legislator. A bill is then drafted and a legislator or legislative committee sponsors that bill. By rule, each bill must be accompanied by a *Statement of Purpose* and a *Fiscal Note*. The new bill is introduced in one house of the legislature by being read on the Order of Business "Introduction and First Reading of Bills."[2] A bill may be introduced by a single member, a group of members, or a standing committee. After a bill's introduction, a standing committee conducts a study of all information that may help determine the scope and effect of the proposed law. There is little information compiled at this point. However, committees in both houses keep informal *committee minutes*.[3] Following this study, the standing committee makes a recommendation; if the bill is "reported out" of committee the bill is placed on "second reading." The bill is automatically on "third reading" except in rare circumstances.

The bill is now ready for debate. The floor sponsor of a bill opens and closes debate on that bill. Once debate is closed, each member present casts a vote. If the bill passes, it is transmitted to the other house of the legislature where it goes through the process again. If both houses pass the bill, it is signed by the President of the Senate, who is the Lieutenant Governor, and the Speaker of the House of Representatives and transmitted to the Governor for signature. However, if a bill is to be amended after consideration by the second house, it is passed to the Committee of the Whole. Once the bill is amended, it begins the process again as with a new bill. Details of a bill's *procedural history* are kept in "Daily Data, Final Edition" (1971–2003) or "Final Weekly Bill Status" (2003–present).

After receiving the bill, the Governor has five days in which to take action by either signing it into law or vetoing it. If the Governor does not sign or veto

---

2. Bills that have been passed by one house are received by the other house and placed on the same Order of Business and treated in the same manner as new bills. Special rules dictate who may introduce bills during certain portions of the legislative session. Ctr. for Pub. Policy & Admin., *Idaho Legislative Manual* at 15; *Idaho Blue Book* at 129–130.

3. The Senate committee minutes have been preserved since 1970; House committee minutes have been preserved since 1960.

a bill, it automatically becomes law. The Governor may issue a statement regarding the legislation whether the bill is signed, vetoed, or allowed to become law without signature. Most bills, however, do not have a *Governor's Statement*. Once a bill has become law, either through signature or without the Governor's approval, it is transmitted to the Secretary of State for assignment of a chapter number in the *Idaho Session Laws*.

The *Idaho Blue Book*[4] contains a detailed explanation of the legislative process in Idaho.[5] It also contains information on the state capitol; a map of legislative districts in Idaho; a list of legislative officers; contact information for legislative staff members; and photographs, biographies, and contact information for Senators and Representatives.

II. Idaho Bill Tracking

Many bills are introduced in each legislative session, and some may affect the rights of a client by proposing new laws or amending existing laws. In advising a client, an attorney needs to learn of any bills on topics relevant to a client's interest and follow their progress through the process outlined above. Table 7-1 outlines the process for bill tracking on the Idaho Legislature's website. This site contains the most up-to-date information and is free; therefore, researchers should use this site to conduct bill tracking research.

Table 7-1. Bill Tracking Online

1. Go to the legislature's website at www.legislature.idaho.gov. Select "Legislative Sessions" and then "Bill Center."
2. When you know the bill number, enter it in the search box.
3. When you do not know the bill number, click on "Legislation by Subject/Topic" and review the subject index.

---

4. This book, the official state directory, is published biennially in odd-numbered years. It is distributed free to libraries, schools, and state agencies in Idaho. It may be accessed online at sos.idaho.gov/elect/bluebook.htm or ordered in print by sending a written request to: Secretary of State's Office, PO Box 83720, Boise, ID 83720-0080.

5. For this more detailed description of how a bill becomes a law, see the *Idaho Blue Book*, at 129–131; www.legislature.idaho.gov/about/howabillbecomesalaw.htm.

A. Researching with a Bill Number

If you know the number of a bill you need to track, you can easily do so on the Idaho legislature's website at no charge.[6] Simply select "Legislative Sessions" from the main page, then "Bill Center." Enter the bill number in the search box. From the resulting list, click on the bill number to access a page that includes the bill text, procedural history, statement of purpose, and fiscal note. You can review where that bill is in the legislative process from the resulting screen, or you can select "Full Bill Information" to read the text of the bill or "Statement of Purpose/Fiscal Note" to access those documents.

B. Learning about Other Pending Bills

If you do not know the bill number, or if you need to learn whether there is pending legislation that affects your work, then research requires an additional step. Select "Legislative Sessions" from the main page, then "Bill Center." Then click on "Legislation by Subject/Topic." This index provides links to pending bills, arranged by topic. Select the bill number following the topic that is relevant to your research. This will take you to the page for that individual bill. You can review where that bill is in the legislative process from the resulting screen, or you can select "Full Bill Information" to read the text of the bill or "Statement of Purpose/Fiscal Note" to access those documents.

III. Idaho Legislative History Research

Legislative history research is the reverse of bill tracking. Bill tracking follows the legislative process forward, from the introduction of a bill to its possible enactment. In contrast, legislative history research works backwards, beginning with an enacted statute. From the statute as it is codified, you will find the session law chapter number, then the bill number, and finally documents produced during the legislative process.

Legislative history research is needed when the meaning of a statute is not clear from the text or context of a statute. It is especially useful for legislation that has not yet been interpreted by the appellate courts in Idaho. When a statute is ambiguous, reviewing the legislative history assists in the effort to determine the legislature's intent in enacting the statute. When involved in litigation where the meaning of a statute is unclear, first see if other statutes or

---

6. The address is www.legislature.idaho.gov.

cases have addressed the ambiguity. If not, you will need to find the available legislative history and refer to it in your briefs.

This section explains the sources of legislative history in Idaho and how to conduct legislative history research. While much recent information is available online, a trip to the state law library,[7] legislative library,[8] or state archives[9] might be necessary.

A. Sources of Idaho Legislative History

Only after 1970 did the legislature begin to create and preserve a more detailed record; prior to that time, little legislative history material is available. Most of the existing early legislative history material is available only from the legislative library in Boise.[10] However, beginning in 1998, some legislative history is now available online. It can be accessed by bill number on the legislature's website. Select "Legislative Sessions" from the first page, then select the appropriate year from the dropdown menu on the resulting page.

A complete legislative history for a recent Idaho law could contain the following: preliminary material, bill text, statement of purpose, fiscal note, procedural history, committee hearings and floor debates, Governor's Statement, and session law text. Not all of these items will have been produced for every bill, however. Table 7-2 outlines each of these materials. The appendices to this chapter provide examples of Idaho legislative history documents.

B. Compiling Idaho Legislative History

1. Review the Source Note for the Statute

The process of compiling legislative history begins with the *source notes* for a statute. These are available online on the legislature's website, Lexis, and Westlaw, or in print in I.C. or W.I.C.A. Therefore, before beginning legislative

---

7. The state law library is located in the Idaho Law & Justice Learning Center in Boise; address and contact information are available on its website at www.isll.idaho.gov.

8. The legislative library is on the first floor of the Capitol building in Boise. Contact information is available on its website at www.legislature.idaho.gov/research/referencelibrary.htm.

9. The state archives are located in the Idaho History Center in Boise. Address and contact information are available on its website at http://history.idaho.gov/idaho-state-archives.

10. Some of the material is available in the state law library in Boise and at the University of Idaho College of Law Library in Moscow.

Table 7-2. Legislative History Documents

Preliminary Material	*Content*: Most preliminary material consists of informal minutes from interim study committees. These committees meet throughout the year to study areas where the legislature determined legislation may be useful or needed. Interim study committees produce informal minutes. *Location*: May be found in *Monthly Matters* (1968–1993), *Legislative Perspective* (1993–present), or Legislative Council and Interim committee minutes. Although rare, for older legislation the Idaho State Archives in Boise may have other materials, such as the findings of a study committee. *Date*: Beginning in 2003, interim committee minutes are also available online.
Bill Text	*Content*: Includes the text of the bill as introduced and any amendments to the bill. Related bills and bills on the same topic that were never formally introduced should also be located if available. *Location*: Bill "binders". *Date*: 1957 to present in print; 1998 and after available online.
Statement of Purpose	*Content*: States the intent of the proposed law. Is not modified as the bill is amended during the legislative process; therefore, it may be at odds with the final legislation. Required to accompany all legislation. *Location*: "Statements of Purpose" *Date*: 1972 to present in print; 1998 and after available online.
Fiscal Note	*Content*: Used to identify the cost to the government of the proposed legislation. Required to accompany all legislation. *Location*: "Statements of Purpose" *Date*: 1972 to present in print; 1998 and after available online.
Procedural History	*Content*: Includes information about the bill as it passes through each stage of the legislative process. *Location*: May be found in *Daily Data*, a weekly publication of the legislature arranged by bill number, or the *House Journal* and *Senate Journal*, a formal record of the technical steps in the legislative process arranged by bill number. *Date*: House bills, 1960 to present; Senate bills, 1970 to present; *Daily Data* available online for bills introduced beginning in 1998; *Journals* available online beginning in 1998.

Table 7-2. Legislative History Documents, *continued*

Committee Hearings	*Content*: Informal minutes of each committee's hearings. *Location*: Committee Minutes *Date*: Senate committee minutes have been preserved since 1970, and some House committee minutes have been preserved since 1960. Available online, 2003 to present.
Governor's Statements	*Content*: Any document or statement made by the Governor regarding the legislation. *Location*: Appear in the *House Journal* and *Senate Journal*. *Date*: 1960 to present for House bills; 1970 to present for Senate bills.
Session Law Text	*Content*: All laws enacted by the legislature are published at the end of each session, designated by year and chapter number. Contains the text of the legislation as passed; is controlling if the text of *Idaho Code* differs. Current editions show additions to or deletions from the code section affected and any preamble making legislative findings. *Location*: *Idaho Session Laws* *Date*: 1890 to present.
Committee Hearings & Floor Debates	*Content*: Recordings of committee hearings and floor debates. *Location*: lso.legislature.idaho.gov/MediaArchive/MainMenu.do. *Date*: 2013 sessions onward.

history research, you must know the code number of the statute you need to research; Chapter 6 explains how to find a relevant statute.

After the text of the statute on the legislature's website the source notes appear in brackets; Lexis lists *History* and Westlaw lists *Credits*. At the end of each statutory section in I.C. is a note in brackets containing *historical citations*; in W.I.C.A., the *history* and *historical citation notes* appear in smaller print immediately following the text of the code section. Table 7-3 shows an example of a source note from the legislature's website. These citations include historical codification citations,[11] citations to codifications that enact or amend the code,

---

11. These citations are helpful for conducting research when statutes have been renumbered.

Table 7-3. Excerpt from *Idaho Code* with Source Notes

18-2407. Grading of theft

Theft is divided into two (2) degrees, grand theft and petit theft.

(1) Grand theft.

***

(b) A person is guilty of grand theft when he commits a theft as defined in this chapter and when:

***

3. The property consists of a check, draft or order for the payment of money upon any bank, or a check, draft or order account number, or a financial transaction card or financial transaction card account number as those terms are defined in section 18-3122, Idaho Code; or

4. The property, regardless of its nature or value, is taken from the person of another; or

***

[I.C. § 18-2407, as added by 1981, ch. 183, § 2, p. 319; am. 1982, ch. 272, § 1, p. 703; am. 1983, ch. 19, § 1, p. 54; am 1987, ch. 84, § 1, p. 158; am. 1994, ch. 132, § 2, p. 301; am. 1994 ch. 346, § 21, p. 1089; am. 1998, ch. 326, § 1, p. 1054; am. 2000, ch. 243, § 1, p. 679; am. 2002, ch. 257, § 1, p. 747; am. 2002, ch. 326, § 1, p. 916.]

Source: *https://legislature.idaho.gov/statutesrules/idstat/Title18/T18CH24/SECT18-2407/*.

and citations to the *Idaho Session Laws*. If there are several citations, these are to the original enactment and subsequent amendments. These source notes set out the year of enactment or amendment, and the chapter number and the page of the session laws where the act begins.[12]

For example, the note [I.C. § 18-2407, as added by 1981, ch. 183, § 2, p. 319 ...] means that the statute was classified by the legislature as I.C. § 18-2407 and first appears in *Idaho Session Laws 1981*, Chapter 183, Section 2. On Lexis and in both I.C. and W.I.C.A., the source notes provide information

---

12. Do not confuse the "chapters" in session laws with "chapters" in the Idaho Code. The session law number provides purely chronological record keeping, while the Idaho Code chapter places an enacted law in topical context with other statutes on similar topics.

Table 7-4. Excerpt from Idaho Session Laws 2002

CHAPTER 326
(S.B. No. 1495)
AN ACT

RELATING TO THEFT; AMENDING SECTION 18-2407, IDAHO CODE, TO FURTHER DEFINE GRAND THEFT....

Be it Enacted by the Legislature of the State of Idaho;

SECTION 1. That Section 18-2407, Idaho Code, be, and the same is hereby amended to read as follows:

18-2407. GRADING OF THEFT. Theft is divided into two (2) degrees, grand theft and petit theft.

(1) Grand theft.

***

(b) A person is guilty of grand theft when he commits a theft as defined in this chapter and when:

***

3. The property consists of a ~~credit card~~ check, draft or order for the payment of money upon any bank, or a check, draft or order account number, or a financial transaction card or financial transaction card account number as those terms are defined in section 18-3122, Idaho Code; or

4. The property, regardless of its nature or value, is taken from the person of another; or

***

Approved March 26, 2002.

Source: *Idaho Session Laws* 2002, pages 916–917.

from the session laws of the Idaho Territory through the most recent amendments and enactments.[13]

---

13. The exception is found in Title 18. Most of the Idaho Criminal Code indicates that it was enacted by Chapter 336 of *Idaho Session Laws 1972*. In 1971, the Idaho Legislature enacted a completely revised criminal code based on the Model Penal Code. The following year, the legislature repealed this code and reenacted the old criminal code. This information is noted in the "compiler's notes" in I.C., but it is not noted in W.I.C.A. Therefore, when conducting legislative history research for statutes in the criminal code, it is necessary to consult I.C. to determine the prior enactments that may affect your analysis. There is no legislative history for the 1972 reenactment.

2. Review the Session Laws

Session laws—the bills in the form in which they were enacted—are published in *Idaho Session Laws*; session laws from 1984 forward are also available on the legislature's website.[14] The bills are organized by session law number, in chronological order based on the date of enactment. The bill number follows the chapter number. Senate bill numbers are preceded by "S.B." and House bills are preceded by "H.B." See Table 7-4. All legislative history research in Idaho is conducted using the bill number; therefore, if a session law is pertinent to your research, note the bill number.

Often a statute will be amended after it is enacted; the historical citations give the session law citation for subsequent amendments.[15] For instance, in Table 7-3 the last citation in the historical citations, [... am. 2002, ch. 326, § 1, p. 916], means that this statute was most recently amended by *Idaho Session Laws* 2002, Chapter 326, Section 1. Table 7-3 also shows numerous other amendments to that statute. Reading each would reveal that I.C. § 18-2407(1)(b)(3) was changed to the current language in 2002. This amendment is illustrated in Table 7-4. Note that in recent *Idaho Session Laws*, such as the one excerpted, deletions are indicated with a strikethrough and additions are shown with underlining.

3. Find the Bill

With the bill number, you can locate the *bill* as it was introduced and any amendments to the bill. Print versions of all bills from 1957 to present are available from the legislative library, arranged by year and bill number in three-

---

14. The address is https://legislature.idaho.gov/statutesrules/sessionlaws/.
15. The historical notes also list prior codifications. These codifications are available in the legislative library and the state law library. They are abbreviated as follows:
C.C.P.: Code of Civil Procedure. These were published as part of the 1881 session laws.
R.S.: 1887 Revised Statutes.
R.C.: 1909 Revised Code of Idaho.
C.L.: Preliminary edition of the 1919 codification. Although not enacted into positive law, this edition follows the Revised Code numbering.
C.S.: 1919 Compiled Statutes.
I.C.A.: 1932 Code Annotated. This code contains notes to similar statutory provisions in other states, and in many cases this information is not noted in the current annotated codes.

ring binders. Beginning with the 1998 legislative session, bills are available on the legislature's website.[16]

4. Find the Statement of Purpose and Fiscal Note for the Bill

Next, in the "Statement of Purpose" volumes, locate both the *statement of purpose* and *fiscal note* for the bill. In print, these volumes are organized by year and bill number; online the statement of purpose and fiscal note are found on the same page as the text of the bill.

5. Find the Procedural History of the Bill

To locate the *procedural history* of a bill, go to either "Daily Data, Final Edition," which covers 1971 to 2003, or "Final Weekly Bill Status," which covers 2004 to the present. These volumes provide a timeline and summary of votes for every introduced bill, arranged in numerical order. For bills introduced in 1998 and after, this information is available online with the bill text.

6. Find the Committee Minutes

Next, find the *committee minutes* relating to the bill. To determine which committees considered the bill, look up the bill number in the "Committee Minute Index" for the appropriate year. The name of each Senate and House committee that considered the bill and the dates on which the bill was discussed are listed. Move next to the Senate and House committee minutes. These bound volumes are arranged first by house, next by year, then by committee, and finally by date. You can locate the discussion of the bill within each date's minutes by finding the bill number in the lefthand column.[17] Beginning in 2003, these minutes are available online.

---

16. Both Lexis and Westlaw provide some Idaho legislative history for recent years, but coverage is limited both by date and content. Lexis's database "Idaho Legislative Bill History" contains House and Senate committee reports, amendments, bill analyses, fiscal amendments, and Governor's Statements. Coverage begins in 2006. "Idaho Advance Legislative Service" includes session laws from 1989 forward. Westlaw's coverage is more limited. It includes only session laws from 1990 forward.

17. The first time a bill is considered, it may be referred to by the number assigned to legislation before it becomes a bill—the routing slip "RS" number. The RS number will be listed next to the bill number in the "Committee Minute Index."

7. Check for Other Sources of Legislative History

In addition to this basic legislative history research, check to see if the bill has a "Statement of Legislative Intent." Very few bills each year will have one of these. The index for these statements is located with the House and Senate *Journals.* Also check to see if the bill was the subject of study by interim committees. The legislative library maintains a list of interim study committees. Check this list for the two years prior to when the bill was introduced. If you find a relevant study committee, you may then read its minutes either in print or online for minutes beginning in 2003. Additionally, beginning with the 2013 session, audio and video recordings of committee meetings and floor debates are available online.

Finally, secondary sources may be helpful in understanding the context surrounding the passage of a bill. The *Idaho Law Review* publishes a "Legislative Review," which examines major legislation passed during the previous session of the Idaho State Legislature. The *Idaho Law Review* also publishes articles on proposed legislation or particular pieces of legislation. The Idaho Bar Association's monthly publication, *The Advocate,* sometimes publishes articles about proposed bills that are of interest to members of the bar. Additionally, the Idaho Bar Association sponsors bills and may publish an explanation of such legislation. Lastly, newspapers published in Idaho sometimes carry articles explaining legislation and quotes sponsors or proponents. You may check local newspapers from bill sponsors' districts for similar articles.

C. Researching Older History

Searching for legislative history prior to 1970 is unlikely to produce many results. Copies of all bills have been kept since 1957, and statements of purpose and fiscal notes have been kept since 1972. Prior to that time, you are likely to find only a record of the technical procedural steps as a bill made its way through the legislative process and session laws. However, check with the legislative library, as some material may be available.

IV. Initiative and Referendum in Idaho

In addition to the traditional method of enacting laws, Idaho's initiative and referendum processes allow for direct legislation by the people of Idaho.[18]

---

18. Idaho Const. art. III, § 1.

The initiative process enables voters to place a measure on the election ballot by collecting a certain number of signatures and meeting other procedural requirements set forth in Title 34, Chapter 18 of the Idaho Code. Through the referendum process, voters may also reject legislation adopted by the state legislature.[19] While this process has become increasingly controversial in recent years,[20] currently in order to appear on a ballot, both an initiative and a referendum require signatures equal to six percent of the number of qualified voters in the last general election.[21]

The Idaho Secretary of State provides many useful resources for understanding the process and the history of initiatives and referendums in Idaho. These materials may be accessed under the "Elections Division" tab of the Secretary of State's website. This site provides the requirements for placing an initiative or referendum on the ballot, as well as a historical listing of all initiatives and referendums placed on Idaho ballots.

V. Attorney General Opinions

In addition to direct legislative history, documents produced by the Attorney General can be used as persuasive authority to convince a court to interpret an ambiguous statute in a way most favorable to your client's position.

The Attorney General is the state's lawyer. In that role, the Attorney General provides formal and informal opinions to the state that are similar to the advice of an attorney to a client. In Idaho, the Attorney General produces three different kinds of documents that may be relevant to legislative history research: formal opinions, informal guidelines (also called informal opinions), and certificates of review.

A formal opinion responds to a specific question posed by the Governor, the Secretary of State, the Treasurer, an agency official, a legislator, or an auditor. As examples, an agency director may ask whether the federal constitution preempts the state constitution in a particular matter, or a senator may ask

---

19. *Id.*
20. For instance, during the 2019 legislative session, the legislature passed HB 296, which would have shortened the time available to gather signatures and increased the needed signatures to ten percent of the qualified electors in the last election in at least two-thirds of the legislative districts. The governor vetoed this bill. https://legislature.idaho.gov/wp-content/uploads/sessioninfo/2019/legislation/H0296-VetoLtr.pdf.
21. I.C. § 34-1805.

about the impact of a statute if enacted. The Attorney General's responses to these questions are published in *Idaho Attorney General's Opinions and Annual Report* and cited by opinion number. They are also available on the Attorney General's website,[22] and on Lexis and Westlaw. Formal opinions are designated by a two-part number. For example, 96-03 was issued in 1996 in response to questions about the effect a tax initiative would have on Idaho's tax structure.

While formal opinions address issues of general concern, informal opinions are likely to affect only the party requesting the opinion. However, some informal opinions deal with proposed legislation. Certain informal opinions are compiled as *Informal Guidelines* and are available in *Idaho Attorney General's Opinions and Annual Report* and on the Attorney General's website. Informal guidelines are designated by the date issued.

Idaho Attorney General's Opinions and Annual Report also publishes certificates of review. By statute, the Attorney General must review all initiative and referendum measures for form, style, and matters of substantive import. After this review, the Attorney General issues certificates of review to the Secretary of State on all initiative and referendum measures.[23] Certificates of review are also designated by the date issued.

Each volume of *Idaho Attorney General's Opinions and Annual Report* provides a separate index for opinions and guidelines, and a table of statutes construed. Some volumes of *Idaho Attorney General's Opinions and Annual Report* also contain a cumulative index of opinions and statutes construed. A ten-year cumulative index is included in the 1985 edition, an eighteen-year index is included in the 1992 edition, a seven-year index is included in the 1999 edition, and a five-year index is included in the 2004 edition. Editions with cumulative indexes note the years covered on the spine. Additionally, the Attorney General's website provides a topical index and a search function, as well as a listing of all opinions, guidelines, and certificates for review by year covering 1975 to present.[24]

---

22. The address is www.ag.idaho.gov/office-resources/opinions/.
23. I.C. § 34-1809.
24. Opinions, guidelines, and certificates of review issued from 1988 on may be accessed online. Simply click on the link provided in the index. Earlier opinions are indexed, but the text is available only in print.

VI. Federal Legislative Research

The legislative process is generally the same at the state and federal levels, but many more materials are available at the federal level. Also, legislative documents have different names or numbering systems at the federal level. For example, federal bills are numbered sequentially in each chamber of Congress. Generally, Senate bill numbers are preceded by an "S," and House of Representatives bill numbers are preceded by "H.R."

A. Federal Bill Tracking

Much congressional material is available from government websites. The Library of Congress website provides bill summaries and status, committee reports, and the *Congressional Record* (which publishes debates in the House and Senate).[25] The Government Publishing Office site contains bills, selected hearings and reports, and the *Congressional Record*.[26] Coverage varies even within a single site, so check carefully.

B. Federal Legislative History

Researching federal legislative history involves roughly the same steps as researching Idaho's laws, though some of the terminology is different. When a federal statute is enacted, it is printed as a small booklet and assigned a *public law number*. This number is in the form Pub. L. No. 101-336, where the numerals before the hyphen are the number of the Congress in which the law was enacted and the numerals after the hyphen are assigned chronologically as bills are enacted. The public law number given above is for the *Americans with Disabilities Act* (ADA), which was passed in 1990 during the 101st Congress.

The new statute is later published as a *session law* in *United States Statutes at Large*, which is the federal counterpart to *Idaho Session Laws*. Session laws are designated by volume and page in *Statutes at Large*, e.g., 104 Stat. 328. Finally, the new statute is assigned a *statute number* when it is codified with statutes on similar topics in the *United States Code*. The citation for the first section of the ADA is 42 U.S.C. § 12101.

As with Idaho legislative history, you must begin federal legislative history research with a statute number. If you do not know the statute number, use

---

25. The website is www.congress.gov.
26. The website is at www.govinfo.gov.

an annotated code to find it as discussed in Chapter 6. With a statute number, you can find the session law citation and public law number, which will lead to the legislative history of the bill as it worked its way through Congress.

1. Sources of Federal Legislative History

In conducting federal legislative history research, you are looking for committee reports, materials from committee hearings, and transcripts of floor debates. Committee reports are considered the most persuasive authority. Unlike Idaho's committee minutes, congressional committee reports are often lengthy documents published in soft-cover format. These reports contain the committee's analysis of the bill, the reasons for enacting it, and the views of any members who disagree with those reasons. Congressional hearing materials include transcripts from the proceedings as well as documents such as prepared testimony and exhibits.

Floor debates are published in the *Congressional Record*. Be wary in relying on these debates as they may not have actually been delivered in the House or Senate; members of Congress can amend their remarks and even submit written statements that are published in transcript form as if they were spoken.

2. Compiled Legislative History

Some researchers have compiled legislative history for certain major federal statutes; therefore, before beginning legislative history research on you own, check to see if the statute's history has already been compiled. A widely known reference book that compiles legislative histories of major federal statutes is *Sources of Compiled Legislative Histories*.[27]

3. Print Sources for Federal Legislative History

Table 7-5 contains the most common print sources for researching federal legislative history. Some sources contain a "How to use" section at the beginning; otherwise, consult a reference librarian.

4. Online Sources for Federal Legislative History

The sites noted earlier in this chapter for tracking federal legislation also provide useful information for legislative history research. The Library of Congress site at provides bill summaries and status, committee reports, and the

---

27. Nancy P. Johnson, *Sources of Compiled Legislative Histories: A Bibliography of Government Documents, Periodical Articles, and Books* (AALL 1979–present) (also available at www.heinonline.org).

7 · BILL TRACKING AND LEGISLATIVE HISTORY

Table 7-5. Selected Sources for Federal Legislative History in Print

Source	Contents
United States Code Congressional and Administrative News (U.S.C.C.A.N.)	Selected reprints and excerpts of committee reports; references to other reports and to the *Congressional Record*
Congressional Information Service (C.I.S.)	Full text of bills, committee reports, and hearings on microfiche; print indexes and abstracts in bound volumes
Congressional Record	Debate from the floor of the House and Senate

Congressional Record. The Government Publishing Office site contains bills, selected hearings and reports, as well as the *Congressional Record*. Much federal legislative history is available on Lexis and Westlaw, both in general databases devoted to legislation and in topical databases. Finally, HeinOnline has several databses with legislative history materials, including the U.S. Code, U.S. Congressional Documents, and the U.S. Federal Legislative History Library.

Appendix.
Examples of Idaho Legislative History

The following pages contain samples of legislative history for the research example used in the legislative history portion of this chapter. These documents are available through the legislative library of Idaho and on the legislature's website. Mistakes in the originals have not been corrected.

Appendix 7-A. Excerpt of Minutes from Senate Committee

Minutes
SENATE JUDICIARY AND RULES COMMITTEE

DATE:	March 6, 2002
TIME:	1:30 pm
PLACE:	Room 437
MEMBERS PRESENT:	Chairman Darrington, Vice Chairman Stegner, Senators Sorenson, Barrutia, Richardson, Davis, Lodge, Dunklin
EXCUSED:	Senator Risch
MINUTES:	**Senator Richardson** made a motion to accept the minutes of March 4 as written. Second was by **Senator Stegner** and the motion was carried by voice vote.

S1495	**Heather Reilly** thanked the committee for putting the bill on the agenda at this late date. Idaho law currently defines theft of a credit card as a felony. This bill clarifies the definition of credit card to make clear that all forms of credit cards are included in the Grand Theft Statute. Some Idaho Courts have held "credit card" includes only VISA or MasterCard type accounts, and excludes store credit accounts, debit cards, and the other types of financial transaction cards. This bill clarifies the grand theft statute to include all forms of financial transaction cards including account numbers.
	In addition, the bill aims to include the theft of checks or checking account numbers under the grand theft statute. Currently under Idaho law, theft of checks would only amount to a misdemeanor in light of the fact that the actual value of checks themselves is under $1000.00. This legislation aims to increase the penalty for theft of checks and/or checking account numbers to a felony.
	In recent years Idaho has seen a large increase in the theft and misuse of checks, financial transaction cards and/or just the associated account numbers. This legislation's intent is to address this type of theft and prevent the huge losses, which invariably occur when the thieves fraudulently use, sell or pass on to others the stolen checks, financial transaction cards or account numbers.
	Wade Spain, Police detective, Boise Police, told the committee that the Idaho Banker's Association is in support of this legislation. Identity fraud is increasing and as much damage can be done with the account number as with the actual credit or debit card. When police have searched, they have found notebooks stacked with credit card numbers, or bank statement numbers. Right now, the police can't do anything about it, and the amount being stolen is into the billions of dollars. Online purchases can also be made, as well as checks made on a computer with stolen credit card numbers. At present time, the only penalty is a misdemeanor. **Pam Eaton**, Idaho Retailers Association spoke in support of S1495.
MOTION:	**Senator Barrutia** made a motion to send S1495 to the floor with a do pass. Second was by **Senator Lodge** and the motion was carried by a voice vote. **Senator Lodge** will carry this bill on the Senate floor.

***

Source: http://legislature.idaho.gov/legislation/2002/S1495.html.

Appendix 7-B. Statement of Purpose

```
        STATEMENT OF PURPOSE
             RS 12157
```

Idaho law currently defines theft of a credit card as a felony. This bill clarifies the definition of credit card to make clear that all forms of credit cards are included in the Grand Theft Statute. The definition comes from Idaho Code 18-3122 (6) and (7) "financial transaction card" (FTC) and "financial transaction card" account numbers. Some Idaho Courts have held "credit card" in 18-2407 includes only VISA or MasterCard type accounts, and excludes store credit accounts, debit cards, and the other types of financial transaction cards. This bill clarifies the grand theft statute to include all forms of financial transactions cards including the account numbers.

In addition, the bill aims to include theft of checks or checking account numbers under the grand theft statute. Currently under Idaho Law, theft of checks would only amount to a misdemeanor in light of the fact that the actual value of checks themselves is under $1000.00. This legislation aims to increase the penalty for the theft of checks and/or checking account numbers to a felony.

In recent years Idaho has seen a large increase in the theft and misuse of checks, financial transaction cards and/or just the associated account numbers. This legislation's intent is to address this type of theft and prevent the huge losses, which invariably occur when the thieves fraudulently use, sell or pass on to others the stolen checks, financial transaction cards or account numbers.

```
            FISCAL IMPACT
```
There is no direct fiscal impact on the general fund

Contact
```
    Name: Heather Reilly
    Phone: (208) 287-7700
```

Source: http://legislature.idaho.gov/legislation/2002/S1495.html.

Appendix 7-C. Online Daily Data Tracking History

S1495....................................by JUDICIARY AND RULES
THEFT—FINANCIAL TRANSACTION CARDS—Amends existing law to further define
grand theft to include the theft of checks, drafts or orders for payment
upon banks, financial transaction cards, or the account numbers relating to
such checks, drafts, orders for payment or financial transaction cards.

```
03/04    Senate intro—1st rdg—to printing
03/05    Rpt prt—to Jud
03/07    Rpt out—rec d/p—to 2nd rdg
03/08    2nd rdg—to 3rd rdg
03/11    3rd rdg—PASSED—35-0-0
   AYES—Andreason, Boatright, Branch(Bartlett), Brandt, Bunderson,
   Burtenshaw, Cameron, Darrington, Davis, Deide, Dunklin, Frasure,
   Geddes, Goedde, Hawkins, Hill, Ingram, Ipsen, Keough, King-Barrutia,
   Little, Lodge, Marley, Noh, Richardson, Risch, Sandy, Schroeder,
   Sims, Sorensen, Stegner, Stennett, Thorne, Wheeler, Williams
   NAYS—None
   Absent and excused—None
   Floor Sponsor—Lodge
   Title apvd—to House
03/12    House intro—1st rdg—to Jud
03/14    Rpt out—rec d/p—to 2nd rdg
03/15    2nd rdg—to 3rd rdg
   Rls susp—PASSED—59-8-3
   AYES—Barraclough, Bedke, Bell, Bieter, Black, Block, Boe, Bolz,
   Bradford, Campbell, Clark, Collins, Cuddy, Deal, Denney, Ellis,
   Eskridge, Field(13), Gagner, Gould, Hadley, Hammond, Harwood,
   Henbest, Higgins, Hornbeck, Jaquet, Jones, Kellogg, Kendell, Kunz,
   Langford, Loertscher, Mader, Martinez, Meyer, Montgomery, Mortensen,
   Pearce, Pischner, Pomeroy, Raybould, Ridinger, Roberts, Robison,
   Sali, Schaefer, Sellman, Shepherd, Smith(33), Smith(23), Smylie,
   Stevenson, Stone, Tilman, Trail, Wood, Young, Mr. Speaker
   NAYS—Barrett, Callister, Crow, Ellsworth, Lake, McKague, Moyle,
   Wheeler
   Absent and excused—Aikele, Bruneel, Field(20)
   Floor Sponsor—Pearce
   Title apvd—to Senate
03/15    To enrol
03/18    Rpt enrol—Pres signed—Sp signed
03/18    To Governor
03/26    Governor signed
         Session Law Chapter 326
         Effective: 07/01/02
```

Source: http://legislature.idaho.gov/legislation/2002/S1495.html.

Chapter 8

Rules of Court and Professional Ethics

Attorneys must work within rules of court and professional ethics. This chapter first discusses court rules, concentrating on court rules in Idaho but also covering federal court rules. The chapter then turns to the ethical rules that govern the conduct of attorneys in Idaho.

I. Court Rules

Court rules govern litigation practice from the filing of the initial pleading through the final appeal. Rules dictate litigation details ranging from the correct caption for pleadings to the standard for summary judgment. Court rules like the Idaho Rules of Civil Procedure are primary authority, and they are promulgated by the Idaho Supreme Court. Success in litigation may depend as much on compliance with these rules as on the merit of the claims.

A. Idaho Court Rules

Court rules cover many topics. See Table 8-1. Idaho court rules are available on Casemaker, Lexis, Westlaw, and other online sources, as well as on the judiciaries' website.[1] Michie publishes *Idaho Court Rules* in two soft-bound, annotated volumes with the code compilation *Idaho Code*.[2] West also publishes a set called *Idaho Court Rules, State and Federal*. The coverage of the print sets differ, so if researching in print be sure to check the coverage.

The process for researching court rules mirrors the process for researching statutes.

---

1. The website is https://isc.idaho.gov/main/idaho-court-rules.
2. In some jurisdictions, volumes such as these are referred to as "deskbooks."

Table 8-1. Idaho Court Rules

Idaho Rules of Civil Procedure	Idaho Infraction Rules
Idaho Rules of Family Law Procedure	Idaho Juvenile Rules
	Idaho Court Administrative Rules
Idaho Rules of Evidence	Idaho Rules of Professional Conduct
Idaho Criminal Rules	Idaho Appellate Rules
Idaho Misdemeanor Criminal Rules	Idaho Rules on Small Claim Actions

B. Reading Rules

Rules are written in outline form like statutes, and they should be read like statutes. Read each word carefully, refer to cross-referenced rules, and scan other rules nearby to see if they are relevant also. After finding a rule on point, use any annotations following that rule to find cases that apply the rule. The annotations on Lexis and in *Idaho Court Rules* contain a comparison to the federal rules; if a federal rule is substantially similar, cases applying it are persuasive authority and may be relevant to your application of the Idaho rule.

C. Federal Court Rules

Similar court rules exist on the federal level. They can be found on various online services. In print, they are published in U.S.C., U.S.C.A., and U.S.C.S. Placement of the rules varies among the statutory publications.[3]

As at the district court level, each court may have its own local rules with specific practices required by that court. Local rules of procedure for the District of Idaho, local bankruptcy rules of procedure for the District of Idaho, and other federal rules affecting Idaho practice are available on the court's website[4] and are printed in volume two of Michie's *Idaho Court Rules*. The U.S. Supreme Court's rules are posted on its website.[5]

Cases relevant to federal rules can be located using the Westlaw or Lexis annotated codes, or by referring to *Federal Practice Digest*, *Federal Rules Service*

---

3. In U.S.C. and U.S.C.A., for example, the Federal Rules of Appellate Procedure appear just after Title 28. In U.S.C.S., those rules are found at the end of all titles in separate volumes devoted to the rules.

4. The address is http://www.id.uscourts.gov/district/forms_fees_rules/Civil_Rules.cfm.

5. The address is www.supremecourt.gov.

(rules of procedure), and *Federal Rules of Evidence Service*. Treatises on federal rules are covered in Chapter 4.

II. Ethical Rules

*A lawyer, as a member of the legal profession,
is a representative of clients, an officer of the legal system
and a public citizen having special responsibility for the quality of justice.*[6]

Idaho attorneys are subject to the Idaho Rules of Professional Conduct. These rules are based on the American Bar Association's Model Rules of Professional Conduct, which have been adopted in varying form in most states.

Idaho's Supreme Court first adopted its version of the model rules in 1986. At that time, the Court did not adopt the comments to the model rules, so any discrepancy had to be resolved in favor of the rules. Over the years, the rules were amended by subsequent orders of the Supreme Court. The most recent amendments to the rules by the Idaho Supreme Court became effective July 1, 2014. The broad topics covered are outlined in Table 8-2.

Table 8-2. Topics of Idaho Rules of Professional Conduct

1. Client Lawyer Relationship
2. Counselor
3. Advocate
4. Transactions with Persons Other than Clients
5. Law Firms and Associations
6. Public Service
7. Information about Legal Services
8. Maintaining the Integrity of the Profession

Idaho's ethical rules are available on the state bar's website,[7] on various online services, and in print in Michie's *Idaho Court Rules*, West's *Idaho Court*

---

6. Idaho Rules of Professional Conduct, Preamble (2003).
7. The address is https://isb.idaho.gov/bar-counsel/irpc/.

Rules, State and Federal and in the most recent version of the Idaho State Bar Desk Book Directory.[8]

The Idaho Supreme Court governs attorney conduct in Idaho. Use the research methods discussed in Chapter 11 to determine how the Idaho Supreme Court has interpreted the Rules of Professional Conduct.

Unlike some other jurisdiction, the Idaho State Bar no longer issues formal ethics opinions. You can find its formal ethics opinions online at https://isb.idaho.gov/bar-counsel/formal-opinions. These opinions don't address the current Rules of Professional Conduct and many have been designated obsolete, disavowed, overruled, superseded by another formal opinion or subsequently addressed by an ABA ethics opinion. The Notes column on the Formal Ethics Opinions List, the front page of the link to these formal ethics opinions, should therefore be consulted with respect to the subsequent treatment of any particular formal opinion. However, the principles addressed in the formal opinions, to the extent they remain applicable and consistent with the current Idaho Rules of Professional Conduct are still utilized to interpreting the current Rules.

---

8. This directory is published each April by the Idaho State Bar as a volume of *The Advocate*. In addition to the Rules of Professional Conduct, it also includes the Idaho Bar Commission Rules, Civility in Professional Conduct Standards, Idaho State Bar Forms, an Idaho Bar membership roster, and contact information for federal and state courts in Idaho, University of Idaho College of Law faculty, Concordia University School of Law faculty, and the Idaho Judicial Council.

Chapter 9

Administrative Law

I. Administrative Law and Governmental Agencies

Administrative law is another source of primary authority. It encompasses the rules and decisions of governmental agencies. The focus of this chapter is Idaho administrative law, though federal administrative law is also considered briefly.

Idaho agencies include boards, commissions, and departments that are part of the executive branch of government.[1] Examples of state agencies in Idaho include the Department of Fish and Game, the Public Utility Commission, and the Board of Education. A list of Idaho state agencies can be found online.[2]

Although agencies are administered by the executive branch, they are established by the legislature through enabling statutes. The statutory provisions that create agencies establish the powers and duties of the agencies; each agency must work within the limits set by its enabling statute or constitutional provision.[3]

Administrative law is primary authority like statutes and cases. It is unique because agencies perform functions of all three branches of government. Agencies write rules that interpret and apply statutes in the agencies' jurisdictions;

---

1. "'Agency' means each state board, commission, department or officer authorized by law to make rules or to determine contested cases, but does not include the legislative or judicial branches, executive officers listed in section 1, article IV, of the constitution of the state of Idaho in the exercise of powers derived directly and exclusively from the constitution, the state militia or the state board of correction." I.C. §67-5201(2).

2. The address is at http://adminrules.idaho.gov/rules/current.

3. The Idaho Constitution allocates agencies among no more than twenty departments and allows for the creation of temporary agencies. Idaho Const. art. IV, §20. The Idaho Constitution also creates the Department of Water Resources and delineates that agency's powers. Idaho Const. art. XV, §7.

these rules are similar in form and in authority to statutes enacted by the legislature. As part of the executive branch, agencies issue licenses (e.g., drivers' licenses) and conduct investigations to see whether laws are being followed (e.g., inspecting environmental sites). Agencies also hold quasi-judicial hearings, deciding cases that involve the agency's rules or its mission (e.g., to suspend a dental license or award unemployment benefits). These hearings are similar to court proceedings, but less formal.

In general, agencies function within the bounds of an Administrative Procedures Act (APA), such as Idaho's Administrative Procedure Act (Idaho APA), found at Title 67, Chapter 52 of the Idaho Code.[4] The Idaho APA requires that the public be involved in developing agency policy and drafting rules. The public may petition agencies for the adoption, amendment, and repeal of a rule.[5] Agencies are encouraged to use negotiated rulemaking, "a process in which all interested persons and the agency seek consensus on the content of a rule[,]" whenever it is feasible.[6] Agencies are required to "afford all interested persons reasonable opportunity to submit data, views and arguments, orally or in writing" prior to the adoption, amendment, or repeal of a rule.[7] To meet this goal, agencies accept public comment for twenty-one days after the notice of proposed rulemaking is published, and must provide an opportunity for public hearings under certain circumstances.[8]

Each of the three branches of government has some oversight of agency functions. The legislative branch generally grants agencies the power to perform their duties and provides funding for the agencies to operate. The courts may determine in contested cases whether agencies' rules are valid. The Governor is the supervisor of all state agencies, and the executive branch exercises control over some agencies by appointing their highest officials.

II. Administrative Rules

Administrative agencies promulgate *rules*, similar to the legislature enacting statutes. Administrative rules are written in an outline-numbering format similar to that of statutes. Rules are defined by Idaho statute as "the whole or a part of an agency statement of general applicability that has been promulgated

---

4. Some agencies are exempt from portions of the Idaho APA. I.C. § 67-5240.
5. I.C. § 67-5230.
6. I.C. § 67-5220(2).
7. I.C. § 67-5222(1).
8. I.C. § 67-5222.

Table 9-1. Example of Idaho Administrative Rule Numbering

IDAPA 38.05.01.074.03.c.ii.

"IDAPA" refers to Idaho Administrative Rules in general that are subject to the Administrative Procedures Act and are required to be published in the *Idaho Administrative Code* and the *Idaho Administrative Bulletin*.

"IDAPA 38." refers to the Idaho Department of Administration.

  "05." refers to Title 05 which is the Department of Administration's Division of Purchasing.

   "01." refers to Chapter 01 of Title 05, "Rules of the Division of Purchasing."

    "074." refers to Major Section 074, "Mistakes."

     "03." refers to Subsection 074.03.

      "c." refers to Paragraph 074.03.c.

       "ii." refers to Subparagraph 074.03.c.ii.

Source: *Idaho Administrative Code*, https://adminrules.idaho.gov/rules/current/38/380501.pdf.

in compliance with the provisions of [the Idaho APA] and that implements, interprets, or prescribes: (a) law or policy; or (b) the procedure or practice requirements of an agency...."[9] Many rules supply details that the legislative branch is not able to include in statutes. Since agencies are the experts in particular legal areas, they are well suited for supplying specific details to general statutes. Rules also may provide guidance based on an agency's understanding of a relevant statute or determine procedural deadlines and format for agency filings.

Although rules and statutes are both primary authority, rules are subordinate to statutes. If there is any inconsistency between a rule and a statute, the statute has priority. Moreover, a rule cannot "cure" a statute that a court has held to be unconstitutional.

Administrative rules in Idaho are designated by a seven-part citation in the form "IDAPA 00.00.00.000.00.x.xx." The first two digits refer to the agency identification number. For instance, "IDAPA 38" refers to the Idaho Department of Administration. The next two digits are the agency division or department title number. The third two-digit number refers to the chapter number. These are followed by the rule citations; rules are divided into major sections (a three-digit number), subsections (the final two-digit number), paragraphs (a letter), and subparagraphs (a roman numeral). See Table 9-1

---

9. I.C. § 67-5201(19).

for an example of Idaho administrative rule numbering. Note that the agency chapter number is not related to the chapter of the Idaho Code that created the agency.

III. Researching Idaho Administrative Law

The basic process for researching Idaho administrative law is outlined in Table 9-2. Realize that the most valuable resource in administrative law research is often the agency itself. While statutes and rules are relatively easy to find, additional policies, regulations, guidance documents, and decisions exist that may be difficult to access. A large part of your research should be talking to the agency's representatives to find out what material is available. For example, a handbook provided by the agency may outline the steps in filing a claim.

Table 9-2. Outline for Idaho Administrative Law Research

1. Find the enabling act, the statutory provision granting the agency power to act. Research case law to determine whether the agency acted within that power.
2. Find the text of the relevant rule in *Idaho Administrative Code* (IDAPA) for the year at issue.
3. Update the rule in the *Idaho Administrative Bulletin* to find any proposed changes. (The Westlaw citator, KeyCite, also provides updating for Idaho rules.)
4. Find agency and judicial decisions applying the rule in similar circumstances.

A. The Enabling Act

Analytically, the initial question with any agency action is whether the agency acted within its power. If that is in doubt, the first step in researching an administrative rule is to find the statute that gives the agency power to act. The next step is to find cases that interpret the statute's provisions. Chapter 6 explains the process of researching statutes. Chapter 11 explains how to find cases in addition to those listed in annotated codes. If the agency's power is clear, skip this inquiry and move directly to finding relevant rules, as explained next.

B. *Idaho Administrative Code*

Idaho's administrative rules are published each July by the Department of Administration, Office of the Administrative Rules Coordinator, in *Idaho Ad-

ministrative Code (known as IDAPA not IAC).[10] IDAPA includes the full text of rules, final or temporary, that are in effect as of *sine die* of that year.[11] Starting in 2010, IDAPA became available online.[12]

Administrative rules are available on the Department of Administration's website.[13] On that site, you can access rules through an alphabetical index of agencies or use a search engine. Idaho administrative rules are available on both Lexis and Westlaw. Both services allow searching either the full text of the rules or the IDAPA table of contents. The information on the State's website, however, is often more current than that provided by these commercial services.

If researching previous versions of IDAPA, the Department of Administration provides an archived code going back to 1996.[14] Westlaw provides archival material dating back to 2002. To find links to the archival material on Westlaw, you need to Browse Idaho materials, select "Idaho Regulations" and then select "Idaho Historical Regulations" from the "Tools & Resources" list on the right-

---

10. Prior to 1993, Idaho did not have a centralized system for publishing rules and updates. Instead, each agency was required to compile, index, and publish all effective rules. These compilations, maintained by the agency and the State Law Library, were the official rules of the agency. Therefore, in order to research rules from prior to 1993, it is necessary to contact the State Law Library. The library has each change and update, so it is possible to reconstruct earlier rules.

11. *Sine die* is the last day of the legislative session. All effective and enforceable rules must be formally promulgated and adopted or extended by the Idaho legislature. I.C. § 67-5291. By statute, every administrative rule expires on July 1 of the year following its adoption or extension; in order to remain effective, the legislature must extend a rule by statute. I.C. § 67-5292.

12. The address is http://adminrules.idaho.gov/rules/current/index.html. While not available in print, you can order a copy of IDAPA and the bulletin on CD Rom from the Department of Administration.

If you are researching rules published prior to 2010, you can choose to research either in print or online. The preface of the print source contains an alphabetical list of agencies and their corresponding agency identification numbers. Each volume of the *Idaho Administrative Code* also contains a subject index for that volume; the *Idaho Administrative Code* does not, however, contain a general index for locating rules on a particular topic. When using only print sources, skim the list of agencies and determine which would be likely to make rules relevant to your client's situation. Turn to that agency's rules in IDAPA and either skim them to see which ones apply or locate the correct volume and use the subject index at the back.

13. They are available at http://adminrules.idaho.gov.

14. The address is https://adminrules.idaho.gov/rules/archive.html.

hand side of the screen. Casemaker provides archival materials dating from the last legislative session back to 2008.

After finding relevant rules, read the text of each rule carefully. Many techniques used for reading statutes apply equally well to reading administrative rules.[15] In particular, always look for a separate rule that provides definitions, be aware of cross-references, read the text several times, and outline any complicated provisions.

Table 9-3 provides an example of an Idaho rule. Note that following the text of each rule is the date of adoption of that rule. This date can be important in determining when a rule was promulgated, amended, or renum-

Table 9-3. Excerpt from an Idaho Rule
IDAPA 02.02.04.050

050. SUMMER APPLES.

***

02. Idaho Summer Extra Fancy. Idaho Summer Extra Fancy shall consist of apples of one (1) variety which are mature, hand-picked, clean, sound, fairly well formed and free from visible watercore, broken skin and from damage caused by insects, disease, mechanical injury or other causes. Each apple shall have the amount of color hereinafter specified for apples in this grade. Caution: To be certified on an Export Form Certificate, all apples must meet U.S. No. 1 grade requirements. Effective Date (7-1-93)

***

c. The following shall not be considered damage. Effective Date (7-1-93)

i. Slight handling bruises or box bruises, such as are incidental to good commercial handling in the preparation of a tight pack. Effective Date (7-1-93)

ii. Sunburn or sprayburn when the normal color of the apple is not seriously affected, and there is no blistering or cracking of the skin, and the discolored area blends into the normal coloring of the apple. Effective Date (7-1-93)

iii. Dark colored limb rubs not to exceed one-half (1/2) inch in the aggregate area. Limb rubs of a light brown or russet character shall be governed by the definition covering solid russeting. Effective Date (7-1-93)

***

Source: *Idaho Administrative Code*, https://adminrules.idaho.gov/rules/current/02/020204.pdf.

---

15. The statutory interpretation framework explained in Chapter 6 applies to administrative rules as well as to statutes. *See Mallonee v. State*, 139 Idaho 615, 619, 84 P.3d 551, 555 (2004).

bered, since a legal issue will be controlled by the rules in effect when the issue arose.

C. *Idaho Administrative Bulletin*

Updates to Idaho rules are published monthly by the Department of Administration, Office of the Administrative Rules Coordinator, in the *Idaho Administrative Bulletin*. The *Bulletin* is available on the State's website. The website contains the current issue of the *Bulletin*, as well as past issues from recent years. The *Bulletin* is available on Lexis under the "Browse Sources" tab; it is not currently available on Westlaw.

1. Updating an Idaho Rule

Updating a rule on the State's website is easy. Access the Cumulative Rulemaking Index using the link on the left side of the screen. Then simply click on the name of the agency. Again, rules that have been affected will be listed along with the date of the *Bulletin* in which the change was published. From there, access the archived *Bulletins*; information is provided from November 1995 to the most current version of the *Bulletin*. Alternatively, you may use the search engine provided to access all rules and *Bulletins* that contain a reference to the rule you are updating.

The versions of IDAPA provided on Lexis and Westlaw incorporate changes through the most recent *Bulletin* that the service has received. If the current *Bulletin* has not yet been received, information on the State's website may be more recent. Typically, the commercial services lag several weeks behind.

2. Other *Bulletin* Information

In addition to providing updated text of rules, the *Bulletin* gives notice of proposed action on rules by various agencies. Agencies must announce when they intend to introduce new rules or modify existing rules. The *Bulletin* lists notices and announcements in "Legal Notice: Summary of Proposed Rulemaking."

Executive orders also are included in the *Bulletin*. As one example, when the Governor declares a state of emergency due to wildfires in an area of the state, his executive order is printed in the *Bulletin*.[16]

---

16. Additionally, beginning in 1975, executive orders may be found in *Idaho Session Laws*.

D. Guidance Documents

In addition to rules, many agencies use "guidance documents" in the administration of their duties. Guidance documents include policy statements, agency manuals, and legal interpretations. Generally, these documents are guidelines and interpretations of agency rules — reference tools for agency employees when dealing with the public. Agencies must index guidance documents and make them available to the public.[17] Guidance documents do not have the force and effect of law, or any precedential authority.[18] However, guidance documents indicate an agency's probable interpretation of a rule or regulation.

The index for a particular agency's guidance documents is available from the agency itself. Contact information for agencies may be found online[19] or in the *Idaho Blue Book*.

E. Agency Decisions

In addition to their rule-making function, agencies also act in a quasi-judicial role, adjudicating cases pertaining to agency rules or actions. There may be several levels of agency review, depending on the agency. The Attorney General has promulgated rules of procedure for contested cases before agencies.[20] However, agencies may adopt different procedures. Check with a particular agency to learn the procedure it follows.

Idaho agencies are encouraged to use informal procedures to resolve contested cases.[21] If a formal procedure is used, the case is heard by a hearing officer; these proceedings may resemble short, informal trials. At the conclusion of the hearing, the hearing officer may issue a final order, preliminary order, proposed order, or recommended order. The identity of the hearing officer partially determines the type of order. If the agency head is the hearing officer, the order is a final order, unless it is issued as a proposed order. If the hearing officer is not the agency head, the order issued may be a preliminary order (which may become final without the agency head's approval) or a recommended order (which requires the agency head's approval after comment from the parties).[22]

---

17. I.C. § 67-5250.
18. I.C. § 67-5250(2).
19. The information is available at www.idaho.gov/agencies/.
20. IDAPA 04.11.01 *et seq*. These rules are commonly referred to as Idaho Rules of Administrative Procedure (IRAP).
21. I.C. § 67-5241; IDAPA 04.11.01.100.
22. I.C. §§ 67-5243 to -5246.

Agency decisions are difficult to find. Most Idaho agencies do not compile their decisions into reporters or publish them.[23] Some agencies make their decisions available online. Most, however, do not. Contact the agency to locate its decisions.

Idaho courts have jurisdiction to review any final agency action.[24] Orders from the Idaho Industrial Commission and Public Utilities Commission are appealed directly to the Idaho Supreme Court.[25] Orders from other administrative agencies may be appealed to district court for review.[26] Conducting case research (see Chapter 11) may reveal cases that address the agency rules and orders relevant to your research.

IV. Researching Federal Administrative Law

The federal government's agencies function much like Idaho's. Agencies such as the Civil Rights Division of the Department of Justice, the Internal Revenue Service, and the U.S. Fish and Wildlife Service are invaluable parts of the executive branch.

The federal APA is codified at 5 U.S.C. §551 *et seq*. Like the Idaho APA, its goals are to promote uniformity, public participation, and public confidence in the fairness of the procedures used by agencies of the federal government.

A. *Code of Federal Regulations*

Federal administrative rules are called *regulations*. Federal regulations are published by the Government Publishing Office (GPO) in the *Code of Federal Regulations* (C.F.R.). This is a codification of regulations issued by federal agencies.

Similar to IDAPA in Idaho, regulations in C.F.R. are organized by agency and subject. The fifty titles of C.F.R. do not necessarily correspond to the fifty titles of the *United States Code* (U.S.C.), although some topics do fall under the same title number. For instance, Title 7 in both C.F.R. and U.S.C. pertain to agriculture, but Title 11 of U.S.C. addresses bankruptcy, while the same

---

23. The Idaho Industrial Commission published its decisions in *Idaho's Worker's Compensation Decisions*, a periodical, from 1981 to 2002. Its decisions beginning in 2010 are available online at http://iic.idaho.gov/decisions/decisions.html.
24. *See* I.C. §§ 67-5270; 67-5278.
25. I.C. §§ 1-2406; 67-5270(3).
26. I.C. §§ 67-5270 to -5279.

Table 9-4. Example of a Federal Regulation

36 C.F.R. 223.2

TITLE 36 — PARKS, FORESTS, AND PUBLIC PROPERTY
CHAPTER II — FOREST SERVICE, DEPARTMENT OF AGRICULTURE
PART 223 — SALE AND DISPOSAL OF NATIONAL FOREST SYSTEM TIMBER
Subpart A — General Provisions

Sec. 223.2 Disposal of timber for administrative use.

Trees, portions of trees, or other forest products in any amount on National Forest System lands may be disposed of for administrative use, by sale or without charge, as may be most advantageous to the United States, subject to the maximum cut fixed in accordance with established policies for management of the National Forests. Such administrative use shall be limited to the following conditions and purposes:

(a) For construction, maintenance or repair of roads, bridges, trails, telephone lines, fences, recreation areas or other improvements of value for the protection or the administration of Federal lands.

(b) For fuel in Federal camps, buildings and recreation areas.

(c) For research and demonstration projects.

(d) For use in disaster relief work conducted by public agencies.

(e) For disposal when removal is desirable to protect or enhance multiple-use values in a particular area.

Source: *https://www.govinfo.gov/content/pkg/CFR-2018-title36-vol2/pdf/CFR-2018-title36-vol2-sec223-2.pdf.*

title in C.F.R. deals with federal elections. See Table 9-4 for an example of a federal regulation.

C.F.R. volumes are updated annually, with specific titles updated each quarter. Titles 1 through 16 are updated as of January 1;[27] Titles 17 through 27 are updated as of April 1; Titles 28 through 41 are updated as of July 1; and Titles 42 through 50 are updated as of October 1. Realize, though, that the updates may only become available months after the schedule indicates. Each year, the covers of C.F.R. volumes are a different color, which makes it easy to tell whether a print volume has been updated. If no changes were made in a particular volume for the new year, a cover with the new color is pasted on the old volume.

To research a topic in C.F.R., you may begin with the general index. Look up your research terms or the relevant agency's name, and then read the reg-

---

27. The exception is Title 3, "The President," which includes executive orders from the previous year. Thus, it is not "updated" in the same way that other titles are.

ulations referenced. It may be more efficient to begin your research in an annotated statutory code that contains references to related regulations for each statute. After finding a statute on point, review the annotations following the statutory language for cross references to relevant regulations; some researchers find that *United States Code Service* or Lexis tends to provide more references to regulations than does *United States Code Annotated* or Westlaw. Look up the citations given and review the regulations. On Lexis or Westlaw, a search in the main search box will retrieve regulations as well as other sources.

The annual edition of C.F.R. from 1996 through the present is also available online through the GPO.[28] The text there is no more current than the print versions, but the site allows searching by keyword, citation, and title. You can also use the GPO site to access the "Electronic Code of Federal Regulations" (e-CFR). The e-CFR is an unofficial compilation of C.F.R. material and *Federal Register* amendments produced by the National Archives and Records Administration's Office of the Federal Register and the GPO. The e-CFR is updated daily. The subscription service HeinOnline also has a full C.F.R. database in .pdf files; if your library subscribes to HeinOnline, you may be able to access C.F.R. through that site. Finally, the C.F.R. is also available on Lexis and Westlaw. The code is kept current by these services, eliminating the need for updating, which is explained below in Section C.

B. *Federal Register*

New regulations and proposed changes to existing regulations are published first in the *Federal Register*, the federal equivalent of *Idaho Administrative Bulletin*. The *Federal Register* is the first print source to publish regulations in their final form when they are adopted (i.e., before they are codified in C.F.R.). In addition to providing the text of regulations, the *Federal Register* also contains notices of hearings, responses to public comments on proposed regulations, and helpful tables and indexes. It is published almost every weekday, with continuous pagination throughout the year. Thus, page numbers in the thousands are common. New regulations and proposed changes to existing regulations are also available two websites; these sites allow users several search options.[29]

Each volume of the *Federal Register* covers a single calendar year, and page numbers reach the tens of thousands in the last few months of the year. The

---

28. The address is www.govinfo.gov/help/cfr.
29. The websites are https://www.federalregister.gov and https://www.regulations.gov.

online version of the *Federal Register* covers the years 1936 to the present.[30] Lexis and Westlaw also include the *Federal Register* dating back to 1936, as does the subscription service HeinOnline.

C. Updating a Federal Regulation

To update a federal regulation in print or on the government's website, begin with a small booklet or the database called *List of CFR Sections Affected* (L.S.A.). As its name suggests, L.S.A. lists all sections of C.F.R. that have been affected by recent agency action. L.S.A. provides page references to the *Federal Register* issues where action affecting a section of C.F.R. is included. If the section you are researching is not listed in L.S.A., then it has not been changed since its annual revision. L.S.A. is published monthly and is available online.[31]

Final updating requires reference to a table at the back of the *Federal Register* called "CFR Parts Affected During [the current month]." (Do not confuse this table with the "CFR Parts Affected in this [Current] Issue" located in the Contents at the beginning of each issue.) Refer to this table in each *Federal Register* for the last day of each month for all the months between the most recent monthly L.S.A. issue and the current date. Also check the most recent issue of the *Federal Register* for the present month. The table contains more general information (whether a "part" has been affected, not a "section"), but will note changes made since the most recent L.S.A. CFR Parts Affected is available online through a link on the L.S.A. website noted above.

D. Decisions of Federal Agencies

Like Idaho agencies, federal agencies hold quasi-judicial hearings to decide cases that arise under the agencies' regulations. Some of these decisions are published in reporters specific to each agency, for example, *Decisions of the Federal Labor Relations Authority* (F.L.R.A.). Increasingly, federal agency decisions are available on agency websites and from Lexis and Westlaw.

---

30. It is available through www.govinfo.gov.
31. It is available through www.govinfo.gov.

E. Judicial Opinions

The case research techniques explained in Chapter 11 will lead to opinions in which federal courts reviewed decisions of federal agencies. Additionally, Shepard's is a useful research tool both for updating federal regulations and for finding cases relevant to regulatory research. Shepard's is available on Lexis; the Westlaw counterpart is KeyCite. Both are explained in Chapter 12 of this book.

Chapter 10

Court Systems and Judicial Opinions

A court's written explanation of its decision in a particular dispute is called a judicial opinion or a case. Cases are published in rough chronological order in books called *reporters*.[1] Some reporters include only cases decided by a certain court; others, like *Idaho Reports*, include decisions from all the appellate courts in a state. Still other reporters include cases from courts within a specific geographic region, for example, the western United States. Some reporters publish only those cases that deal with a certain topic, such as bankruptcy or federal procedural rules.[2] Reporters that publish cases from a particular court or geographic region are the most commonly used by general practitioners and are the focus of this chapter. Even if you do all of your research online, case citation formats and pagination will reference print reporters, so it is important to be familiar with this source.

This chapter first provides an overview of the Idaho and federal court systems. It then explains reporters that include Idaho and federal cases.

I. Court Systems

The basic court structure includes a trial court, an intermediate appellate court, and an ultimate appellate court, often called the "supreme" court.[3] These courts exist at both the state and federal levels.

---

1. Chapter 11 explains how to find and read judicial opinions.
2. Examples of topical reporters include *Bankruptcy Reporter* and *Federal Rules Decisions* (federal trial court cases that analyze federal rules of civil and criminal procedure).
3. For brevity, the following description omits the five tribal courts located in Idaho and Idaho Water Adjudications. Basic information on the tribal courts and links to information on each of the tribal courts is available at www.isc.idaho.gov/tribal-state/tribalcourt. Information on the Idaho Water Adjudications may be found at www.srba.state.id.us.

A. Idaho Courts

Idaho has a unified court system; all courts are supervised and administered by the Idaho Supreme Court, which is the head of the judicial branch of the Idaho government.

In Idaho, the trial courts are called district courts. Idaho's forty-four counties are divided into seven judicial districts.[4] Each district has district judges and magistrate judges. District judges hear felony criminal cases and certain civil cases, while magistrate judges hear misdemeanor criminal cases and certain civil cases.

The Idaho Court of Appeals is the intermediate court.[5] Located in Boise, the Court of Appeals is composed of four judges. Panels of three judges on the Idaho Court of Appeals sit to hear cases. If a judge is recused, then another Court of Appeals judge or a current or retired judge sits *pro tempore* to hear the case.

The Supreme Court of Idaho, also located in Boise, has five justices.[6] Unlike most other state supreme courts, the Supreme Court of Idaho still "rides circuit." During its nine-month term, the Court will hear cases in Boise, Lewiston, Idaho Falls, Pocatello, Twin Falls, Moscow, and Coeur d'Alene.[7] The five justices also sit *en banc* to hear all cases, unless a justice is recused and a judge *pro tempore* sits with the court. The *pro tem* judge could be a current trial court judge or a retired Supreme Court justice.

The website for the Idaho judiciary contains helpful information including links to each of the judicial districts, lists of court personnel, recent opinions of the appellate courts, and information on the administration of the Idaho court system.[8]

---

4. A map showing the division of these counties appears in each volume of *Idaho Reports* beginning with Volume 91.

5. Prior to 1982, Idaho's judicial system consisted of two tiers: trial courts and the Idaho Supreme Court. In 1980, a three-tier system was created with the establishment of the intermediate Court of Appeals, which became operational in 1982.

6. A jurist on the highest court is called a "justice," while on lower courts the term "judge" is used.

7. Article V, Section 8, of the Idaho Constitution requires the Idaho Supreme Court to hold at least two terms annually in Lewiston. Idaho Code § 1-208 dictates that the Court hold terms in Coeur d'Alene, Pocatello, Twin Falls, and Lewiston.

8. The website is www.isc.idaho.gov.

B. Federal Courts

In the federal judicial system, the trial courts are called United States District Courts. There are ninety-four district courts in the federal system, with each state having at least one district and some having more. States with relatively small populations, like Idaho, Montana, and Wyoming, may not be subdivided into multiple federal districts. The entire state of Idaho[9] makes up the federal District of Idaho, but the court hears cases in four cities: Boise, Pocatello, Moscow, and Coeur d'Alene.[10] States with larger populations and higher caseloads are subdivided into more districts. For example, California has four federal districts: northern, central, southern, and eastern. Washington has two federal districts: eastern and western.

Intermediate appellate courts in the federal system are called United States Courts of Appeals. There are courts of appeals for each of the thirteen federal circuits. Twelve of these circuits are based on geographic jurisdiction. Eleven numbered circuits cover all the states; the twelfth is the District of Columbia Circuit. The thirteenth federal circuit, called the Federal Circuit, hears appeals from district courts in all circuits on issues related to patent law and from certain specialized courts and agencies.[11]

Idaho is in the Ninth Circuit, so cases from the United States District Court for the District of Idaho are appealed to the United States Court of Appeals for the Ninth Circuit. The Ninth Circuit is the largest of the thirteen federal circuits; in addition to Idaho, it also encompasses Alaska, Arizona, California, Hawaii, Montana, Nevada, Oregon, and Washington, as well as Guam and the Northern Mariana Islands.[12]

The highest court in the federal system is the Supreme Court of the United States. It decides cases concerning the United States Constitution and federal statutes. This court does not have the final say on matters of purely state law; that authority rests with the highest court of each state. Parties who wish to have the U.S. Supreme Court hear their case must file a petition for *certiorari*, as the Court has discretion over which cases it hears.[13]

---

9. The small portion of Idaho that makes up the western edge of Yellowstone National Park is in the District of Wyoming.

10. Information on the District of Idaho may be found at www.id.uscourts.gov.

11. A map showing the federal circuits is available at www.uscourts.gov the Court Websites Links.

12. Information on the Ninth Circuit is available at www.ca9.uscourts.gov.

13. Information on the United States Supreme Court may be found at www.supremecourt.gov.

The website for the federal judiciary contains maps, court addresses, explanations of jurisdiction, and other helpful information.[14]

C. Courts of Other States

Like Idaho and the federal judiciary, most states have a three-tier court system. A few, however, do not have an intermediate appellate court. Another difference in some court systems is that the "supreme" court is not the highest court. In New York, the trial courts are called supreme courts and the highest court is the Court of Appeals; Maryland also calls its highest court the Court of Appeals. Two other states, Massachusetts and Maine, call their highest court the Supreme Judicial Court.

Court websites and citation manuals are good references for learning the names and hierarchy of the courts, as well as for learning proper citation to legal authorities. The two most popular are the *ALWD Guide to Legal Citation*, written by Coleen M. Barger and the Association of Legal Writing Directors,[15] and *The Bluebook: A Uniform System of Citation*, written by students from several law schools.[16] Appendix 1 of *ALWD* and Table I of the *Bluebook* provide information on federal and state courts.

II. Idaho Judicial Opinions

A. Reporters for Idaho Cases

Idaho Reports is the official reporter for Idaho appellate cases. All cases decided by the Idaho Supreme Court and some cases decided by the Idaho Court of Appeals are published together in *Idaho Reports*.[17] Cases from these courts are also reported in a commercially produced regional reporter called *Pacific*

---

14. The address is www.uscourts.gov.
15. ALWD & Coleen M. Barger, *ALWD Citation Guide to Legal Citation* (6th ed., Aspen Publishers 2016) ("*ALWD*"). Most citations in this book conform to *ALWD* unless there is a clear preference in Idaho for a different form.
16. *The Bluebook: A Uniform System of Citation* (The Columbia Law Review et al, ed., The Harvard Law Review Assn. 2016).
17. About fifteen percent of the opinions of the Court of Appeals are published. Many of its opinions are unpublished and are not to be cited as authority; these cases tend to simply apply well-established law. The names of these cases appear in the "Cases Reported" section of *Idaho Reports* and the docket numbers, date of decision, and disposition appear in tables located within *Idaho Reports*. Cases from state trial courts in Idaho are not published; in fact, few states publish opinions at the trial court level. Unpublished opinions may be obtained directly from the court that decided the case.

Reporter, published by West. The text of a court's opinion is the same in the official and unofficial reporters. Beginning with volume 91 of the *Idaho Reports*, additional editorial enhancements (explained below) are also identical for Idaho cases reported in *Idaho Reports* and *Pacific Reporter*.

B. West's Regional Reporters

Commercial reporters often combine several courts' opinions under a single title. *Pacific Reporter* publishes cases from the courts of the following fifteen states: Alaska, Arizona, California, Colorado, Hawaii, Idaho, Kansas, Montana, Nevada, New Mexico, Oklahoma, Oregon, Utah, Washington, and Wyoming.[18] *Pacific Reporter* includes cases from the intermediate and highest appellate courts of most of these states.[19] Other regional reporters are *North Eastern Reporter*, *Atlantic Reporter*, *South Eastern Reporter*, *Southern Reporter*, *South Western Reporter*, and *North Western Reporter*. The states whose cases are included in each of these regional reporters are listed in Table 10-1.

All of these regional reporters are published by West. Because West decided which states to group together in regional reporters, these groupings have no legal impact. In fact, because states were grouped into reporters during the 1800s, some placements now seem nonsensical, for example, placing Kansas cases in the *Pacific Reporter* and Kentucky cases in the *South Western Reporter*.

The coverage of each West regional reporter is not the same as the composition of the federal circuits explained above. The Ninth Circuit includes Alaska, Arizona, California, Hawaii, Idaho, Montana, Nevada, Oregon, and Washington, as well as Guam and the Northern Mariana Islands. It does not include Colorado, Kansas, New Mexico, Oklahoma, Utah, or Wyoming, yet those states' cases are reported in *Pacific Reporter*.

Reporters are published in *series*. In 1931, after volume 300 of *Pacific Reporter* was published, the publisher started a new series called *Pacific Reporter, Second*

They may also be available online through commercial providers of computerized legal research.

18. If a state does not publish its own reporter, the regional reporter may be the official reporter. For example, the official reporter of Alaska cases is *Pacific Reporter*. The publisher, West, also publishes an offprint of *Pacific Reporter* that contains only Alaska cases. It is called *Alaska Reporter*. The appearance, pagination, and editorial aids are exactly like those in *Pacific Reporter*, but the volumes contain only those pages that report cases from Alaska courts.

19. Since 1960, opinions of California's intermediate appellate courts have been published in *California Reporter*, not in *Pacific Reporter*.

Table 10-1. Regional Reporters and States Included

Atlantic Reporter (A., A.2d)	Connecticut, Delaware, District of Columbia, Maine, Maryland, New Hampshire, New Jersey, Pennsylvania, Rhode Island, and Vermont
North Eastern Reporter (N.E., N.E.2d)	Illinois, Indiana, Massachusetts, New York, and Ohio
North Western Reporter (N.W., N.W.2d)	Iowa, Michigan, Minnesota, Nebraska, North Dakota, South Dakota, and Wisconsin
Pacific Reporter (P., P.2d, P.3d)	Alaska, Arizona, California, Colorado, Hawaii, Idaho, Kansas, Montana, Nevada, New Mexico, Oklahoma, Oregon, Utah, Washington, and Wyoming
South Eastern Reporter (S.E., S.E.2d)	Georgia, North Carolina, South Carolina, Virginia, and West Virginia
South Western Reporter (S.W., S.W.2d, S.W.3d)	Arkansas, Kentucky, Missouri, Tennessee, and Texas
Southern Reporter (So., So. 2d, So. 3d)	Alabama, Florida, Louisiana, and Mississippi

Series (abbreviated P.2d). In 2000, following publication of volume 999 in the second series, a third series was started, *Pacific Reporter, Third Series* (abbreviated P.3d). To find a case cited to a reporter with multiple series, you must know which series the case was reported in.

C. Citing Idaho Cases

The abbreviation for *Idaho Reports* is "Idaho." The case *State v. Jeppesen*, 138 Idaho 71, 57 P.3d 782 (2002), can be found in volume 138 of the series *Idaho Reports*, starting on page 71, and in volume 57 of *Pacific Reporter, Third Series*, starting on page 782. The case was decided in 2002 by the Idaho Supreme Court. The case *State v. Perkins*, 135 Idaho 17, 13 P.3d 344 (Ct. App. 2000), can be found in volume 135 of the series *Idaho Reports*, starting on page 17, and in volume 13 of *Pacific Reporter, Third Series*, starting on page 344. The case was decided by the Idaho Court of Appeals in 2000.

Idaho custom dictates that documents filed in Idaho courts use citation to both reporters, called *parallel citation*. Likewise, custom dictates that only the year the court decided the case appear in the parenthetical of Supreme Court cases and that the Idaho Court of Appeals be abbreviated Ct. App. in the parenthetical for intermediate appellate cases.

> EXAMPLES: *State v. Jeppesen*, 138 Idaho 71, 57 P.3d 782 (2002).
>
> *State v. Perkins*, 135 Idaho 17, 13 P.3d 344 (Ct. App. 2000).

When writing a memo or brief in other states, you may choose to cite Idaho cases only to *Pacific Reporter*, if no rule or custom dictates that you must cite to a specific reporter. If you were writing a memo for a firm in Salt Lake City or Seattle, for example, you would cite the Idaho cases mentioned above in *Pacific Reporter, Third Series*. To indicate which state's courts decided the cases, include an abbreviation at the beginning of the date parenthetical. Note that when the name of the jurisdiction is not clear from the reporter, more specific information is needed in the parenthetical. In the second example below, "Idaho Ct. App." replaces "Ct. App." because *Pacific Reporter* contains cases from many jurisdictions.

> EXAMPLES: *State v. Jeppesen*, 57 P.3d 782 (Idaho 2002).
>
> *State v. Perkins*, 13 P.3d 344 (Idaho Ct. App. 2000).

D. Parts of a Reported Case

A reported case contains the exact language of the court's opinion. Additionally, some publishers add supplemental information intended to aid researchers in learning about the case, locating the relevant parts of the case, and finding similar cases. Some of these research aids are gleaned from the court record of the case while others are written by the publisher's editorial staff. The following discussion explains the information and enhancements included in *Idaho Reports*. Most reporters — as well as online resources — will include most of these items, though perhaps in a different order.

To best understand the following discussion, access the case *State v. Jeppeson*, 138 Idaho 71, 57 P.2d 782 (2002) on Lexis or Westlaw by entering *138 Idaho 71* in the main search box or refer to page 71 in volume 138 of *Idaho Reports*.

Parallel Citations. Each case in *Idaho Reports* begins with a parallel citation. Often publishers will provide citations to other reporters that have published the same case. The text of an opinion reported at parallel citations is identical, although some of the editorial enhancements may be different. Beginning with volume 91 in 1966,[20] *Idaho Reports* is reprinted from *Pacific Reporter*, and the editorial enhancements are the same in the two reporters.

Parties and Procedural Designations. All of the parties are listed with their procedural designations. In general, if a losing party has a right to appeal, she will be called the *appellant* and the opposing party will be called the *respondent*.[21] In special proceedings, the party prosecuting the action is the *petitioner* and the opposing party will be the *respondent*.

Docket Numbers. The number assigned to the case by a court is called a docket number. Each court will assign a different docket number to the case, just as each college or university you attended may have assigned you a different student identification number. Docket numbers are helpful in locating the parties' briefs, a court's orders, or other documents related to that case. Because some of these documents are not published, they can be obtained from the court that decided the case or on some websites. To request these documents, you must have the appropriate docket number or, in some instances, the parties' names.

Term of Court and Dates. Each case shows the court that heard the case, the term the case was argued, and the date the case was decided. For citation purposes, only the court that heard the case and the year the case was decided are important.

Background and Holdings. One of the most helpful research aids included by the publishers is this short summary of the key facts, procedure, legal points, and disposition of the case. Reading the background and holdings can quickly tell you whether a case is on point. You cannot rely exclusively on this summary beyond simply determining whether a case might be relevant. Moreover, you must never cite this synopsis, even when it gives an excellent summary of the case, since it is not authoritative.

Background and Holdings also contains procedural information such as the court from which the case was appealed and the judge who wrote the decision. Note that following a judge's name will be "C.J." for the chief justice or judge, or "J." for another justice or judge.

Disposition. The disposition of the case is the court's decision to affirm, reverse, remand, or vacate the decision below. If the appellate court agrees with

---

20. Volume 91 covers cases decided from 1966 to 1968. However, volume 90 also covers cases decided in 1966 and volume 92 covers cases decided in 1967 to 1969.

21. In other jurisdictions, the term "appellee" is used for "respondent" in this situation.

only part of the lower court's decision, the appellate court may affirm in part and reverse in part.

Headnotes. A headnote is a sentence or short paragraph that sets out a single point of law in a case. Most cases will have several headnotes. The text of each headnote often comes directly from the text of the opinion. But because only the opinion itself is authoritative, do not rely on headnotes in analyzing the case and do not cite them in legal documents. At the beginning of each headnote is a number identifying it in sequence with other headnotes. Within the text of the opinion, the same sequence number will appear in brackets at the point in the text supporting the headnote. You should read and cite that text, not the headnote.

Headnotes are generally the product of a given reporter's editorial staff, even when the text of the headnote is identical to language used in the opinion. Thus, the number of headnotes — and the text of the headnotes — may differ depending on which publisher's reporter is being used or which online service you are using. Fortunately, in Idaho the headnotes of the official reporters and the headnotes of West's *Pacific Reporter* are essentially the same for volumes 1 through 90 of the *Idaho Reports* and identical beginning with volume 91. Moreover, the headnotes in West's *Pacific Reporter* will be the same as those on Westlaw. Headnotes used on Lexis, though, will be different.

Procedural Information. Following the headnotes, the attorneys who argued for each party are listed.

Opinion. In *Idaho Reports,* the actual opinion of the court begins after the name of the authoring judge, with the name of that judge given in all capital letters. If no judge is given credit as author of the court's opinion, then the case was decided *per curiam,* and those words directly precede the opinion.

Following the opinion are the votes of the other judges who heard the case. If the judges who heard the case did not agree on the outcome or the reasons for the outcome, there may be several opinions. The opinion supported by a majority of the judges is called the *majority opinion.* An opinion written to agree with the outcome but not the reasoning of the majority is called a *concurring opinion.* In a *specially concurring opinion,* the judge may agree with the reasoning, but write to add more. Opinions written by judges who disagree with the outcome supported by the majority of the judges are called *dissenting opinions.* While only the majority opinion is binding precedent, the other opinions provide valuable insights and may be cited as persuasive authority. If there is no majority on both the outcome and the reasoning, the case will be decided by whichever opinion garners the most support and is called a *plurality decision*.

E. Tables in Idaho Reports

Each volume of *Idaho Reports* contains several helpful tables. Judges serving on the Supreme Court, Court of Appeals, and district courts during the time of the cases reported in each volume are listed in tables at the front of the volume. Elected state officials serving during the time of the cases reported are also listed. *Idaho Reports* includes a map showing the division of Idaho counties into judicial districts and a list of all the attorneys admitted to practice during the time of the cases reported in each volume. Additionally, memorial resolutions appear at the beginning of the *Idaho Reports*.

Each volume contains an alphabetical listing of all the cases reported in that volume. Each case listed indicates which court heard that case and shows the page on which that opinion begins. Any cases decided without a published opinion also appear, followed by "(Table)."[22]

Finally, at the beginning of each reporter is a "Words and Phrases" section. The words or phrases that a court defined in a case appear in bold, followed by the case citation. After the reported cases is a key number digest section, summarizing the topics and key numbers for headnotes of cases in that volume. Chapter 11 explains how to use this topical connectivity to find other cases on the same topic.

F. Slip Opinions and Advance Sheets

The bound volumes of reporters can take months to be published. To make cases available sooner, the Idaho Supreme Court, Idaho Court of Appeals publish *slip opinions* on the judiciary's website under the "Supreme Court Appeals" link. A *slip opinion* is the actual document produced by the court, without the editorial enhancements normally added by the publisher. All opinions are published on this website on the day of release.

Some publishers supply subscribers with *advance sheets*. These are softbound booklets, which can be published much more quickly than hardbound books. *Idaho Reports* does not publish advance sheets, but a commercial service is

---

22. Additionally, a table of statutory provisions construed was included in *Idaho Reports* until volume 134 in 2000.

available for the Idaho appellate courts. The *Idaho Supreme Court Report* (*ISCR*) and *Idaho Court of Appeals Report* (*ICAR*) are published every two weeks in one booklet. The pagination and citation are different from that which will appear in the bound volume of the *Idaho Reports*. However, cases published in the advance sheets may be cited in legal documents filed in any Idaho court, using the citation form noted at the beginning of each opinion.

In addition to cases, each advance sheet contains a list of decisions with synopses of each case, a statute index, and two cumulative tables of cases. One case table is chronological and one is alphabetical; both index the *ISCR*, *ICAR*, reporter citations, rehearing petitions, substitute opinions, and other similar information for each case.

G. Idaho Cases Online

Many online providers make Idaho opinions available online. More details about how to access cases using a citation is provided in the next chapter.

III. Federal Cases

This chapter has dealt with reporters and other sources for the judicial opinions of Idaho and other states. This part explains the reporters and additional sources for cases decided by federal courts. Table 10-2 lists the federal court reporters, along with their citation abbreviations.

Table 10-2. Reporters for Federal Court Cases

Court	Reporter Name	Abbreviation
U.S. Supreme Court	*United States Reports* (official)	U.S.
	Supreme Court Reporter	S. Ct.
	United States Supreme Court Reports, Lawyers' Edition	L. Ed. or L. Ed. 2d
U.S. Courts of Appeals	*Federal Reporter*	F. or F.2d or F.3d
U.S. District Courts	*Federal Supplement*	F. Supp. or F. Supp. 2d

A. Sources for United States Supreme Court Cases

Decisions of the United States Supreme Court are reported in *United States Reports*, which is the official reporter; *Supreme Court Reporter*, which is a West publication; and *United States Supreme Court Reports, Lawyers' Edition*, another unofficial reporter now in its second series and published by Lexis. Although *United States Reports* is the official reporter, meaning that you should cite it if possible, that series frequently publishes cases several years after they are decided. Thus, for recent cases, lawyers often cite the *Supreme Court Reporter*. Another source for finding recent cases from the Supreme Court is *United States Law Week*. This service publishes the full text of cases from the Supreme Court and provides summaries of important decisions of state and federal courts.

There are a number of online sources for U.S. Supreme Court opinions. The Court's website includes slip opinions soon after the decisions are rendered.[23] Many other online sites provide quick access to U.S. Supreme Court opinions as well.

B. Sources for United States Courts of Appeals Cases

Cases decided by the federal intermediate appellate courts are published in *Federal Reporter*, now in its third series. Some Courts of Appeals cases that were not selected for publication in *Federal Reporter*, and may be of limited precedential value, may be published in *Federal Appendix*. Limited access to recent opinions is available on the U.S. Courts website. Some online sites also provide access to these cases. Be careful, however: both of these services provide access to cases that are "unpublished." If a case does not have a citation to the *Federal Reporter*, the case may be of limited authority in some jurisdictions.[24]

C. Sources for United States District Courts Cases

Selected cases from the United States District Courts, the federal trial courts, are reported in *Federal Supplement* and *Federal Supplement, Second Series*. Some online sites also provide access to these cases.

---

23. The address is www.supremecourt.gov/opinions/opinions.aspx.

24. *See e.g.* Fed. R. App. P. 32.1 (authorizing litigants in the federal courts of appeals to cite unpublished opinions of those courts beginning in 2007, but allowing courts to determine the weight of unpublished opinions).

Chapter 11

Researching Judicial Opinions

Lawyers can research judicial opinions in a variety of ways.[1] It might be tempting to jump into researching opinions using a google type search on a premier online service. Keep in mind, however, that there are millions of cases already published and over a hundred-thousand new cases are published every year. Keep in mind also, that an ill-conceived search for judicial opinions on Westlaw or Lexis is expensive. For that reason, be strategic in approaching case law research. Remember how legal information is structured and the information you have at the beginning of your research to construct an effective, efficient search. Once you have found a relevant case, leverage the topical connectivity that publishers provide.

I. Find by Citation

If you have a case citation from your supervisor, a colleague, the filings from your opponent, or from your research into secondary sources, simply enter the citation into the main search bar of any online service. Once you have the relevant case, you can use that case to find other cases by reading the cases cited within that case, finding later cases that cite back to that case, and finding other cases on the same topic. Lexis and Westlaw provide the best topical connectivity. Thus, when beginning a research project with a citation to a relevant case, using one of these services is preferred to using a service without the connectivity.

---

1. Other ways of researching cases are discussed in other chapters: annotated statutory codes list cases that interpret or apply each statute (Chapter 6) or constitutional provision (Chapter 5); citators list cases that analyze an authority known to address the topic of the current project (Chapter 12); and secondary sources that deal with the topic refer to cases either in text or in footnotes (Chapter 4).

Table 11-1. Conducting Effective Natural Language Searches for Judicial Opinions

- **Limit by Jurisdiction**: Focus the results to mandatory cases in Idaho, by clicking on "Explore Content" and then "Idaho" on Lexis; or by clicking "State Materials" and then "Idaho" on Westlaw.
- **Select Terms Carefully**: Take the time to develop research terms as explained in Chapter 2 and 3; consider putting terms of art in quotation marks.
- **Limit Results to Cases**: In Lexis, select a case-law only database such as "Idaho State Cases, Combined." Click on "cases" on the left-hand side of the screen from the results page on Westlaw.
- **Use Filters**: Consider limiting the results by court, date, practice area, or other criteria.
- **Review Numerous Results**: Take the time to carefully review the results. The algorithm can't determine which case is most relevant to you, so don't expect the most relevant case to be among the first several results.

II. Using Search Terms

A. Natural Language Searching

Natural language searching is akin to the google type searching you may do in non-legal contexts. You simply type a search into the search box and get results. To do this type of searching efficiently, however, requires an understanding of the database searching provided. All providers keep their algorithms under wraps. We know, however, that the algorithms can include code to return terms to their root or to use synonyms for the terms; to prioritize certain results; and to leverage their unique content and classification systems.[2] Table 11-1 provides effective techniques for conducting natural language searches.

---

2. Susan Nevelow Mart, Results May Vary In Legal Research Databases, A.B.A. J., March 2018, http://www.abajournal.com/magazine/article/results_vary_legal_research_databases; Lexis Advance: Understanding the Technology & Search Algorithm, https://www.lexisnexis.com/infopro/keeping-current/b/weblog/archive/2013/10/16/lexis-advance-174-understanding-the-technology-amp-search-algorithm.aspx; WestSeach: The World's Most Advance Legal Search Engine, https://lscontent.westlaw.com/images/content/WestSearch%20on%20Westlaw.pdf.

B. Terms-and-Connectors Searching

Terms-and-connectors searching works better late in the case-finding portion of research, especially when researching in an unfamiliar area of the law. Efficient terms-and-connector searching requires a contextual understanding of the area of law to review the number cases produced.

Terms-and-connectors searching, also known as Boolean searching, is more precise than natural language searching. Natural language searching will always produce results, regardless of the order of the terms. Terms-and-connectors searching will generate only results that meet the specific criteria of the search. Chapter 3 provides more guidance on constructing terms-and-connector searches.

III. Leveraging Topical Connectivity: Digests

Digests are topical subject indexes for case law. Once a case is published, the editors add headnotes for each point of law decided in the case. This point of law is then categorized by broad topic, i.e. "Marriage and Cohabitation," and specific topic, i.e., "Agreements Concerning Marriage." These headnotes appear at the beginning of cases, and they are compiled into online databases and print volumes. Originally, digests were published in print by West using the Key Number system to organize the volumes of a digest. This system is now available online through Westlaw; Lexis has a comparable tool.

Digests are powerful research tools because they allow researchers to access every case that covers a certain topic. Online, once you have found a case that is on point, you will see that every headnote is linked to that service's online digest system. Clicking on that link will produce a list of the cases that address that same topic.

You can also access the digest system earlier in the research process. The topic searching tool on Lexis is available under the "Browse" tab at the top of the screen. It includes two options to begin searching. First, you may select "Topics" from the dropdown menu and then type in a request in the "Find a topic," box. Lexis will search its different topic areas and provide a list of those that seem relevant, along with the number of results under each topic. When you find a relevant topic, click on its link and then select "Get documents" to find the resulting documents.

Second, you may click on any one of the listed topics, beginning with broad categories like "Criminal Law & Procedure," "International Law," and "Trademark Law." Each click narrows the topic of the search. When you reach the end of the outline tree, clicking on "Get documents" will take you to the resulting documents.

On arriving at the resulting documents, you may select between sources such as cases, statutes, or administrative materials along the top of the page, or narrow down the jurisdiction on the left side of the page.

On Westlaw, the tool is called "Key Numbers," which is available under "Content types" on the home screen. On Westlaw, each West topic has been assigned a number. For example, Larceny is topic 234. The initial screen shows a list of broad topics like "Criminal Justice," "Education," and "Child Custody." Clicking on a topic reveals a list of subtopics, allowing you to choose more specific terms as you narrow down to the issue you are researching. As an example, to research the intent needed to establish the crime of larceny for someone who stole a purse, click on "Larceny 234," then "I. Offenses and Responsibility Therefor," and "Intent." You can select any subtopic simply by clicking on it or simply search for a term, like *purse* from the resulting screen.

Westlaw will then display search results. Here you can select a jurisdiction for your search and decide whether you want to review only cases with headnotes. The results list screen provides the option of adding terms to the search to narrow its scope in the left-hand frame. Continuing with the example above, you may choose to narrow the search to cases on *intent* and involving *purse*.

IV. Reading and Analyzing Cases

After locating a case in a reporter or online, you must read it, understand it, and analyze its potential relevance to the problem you are researching. This process may take more mental work than you have ever dedicated to a few pages. It is not unusual for a lawyer to spend hours reading a complex case. For a novice, this reading is frequently interrupted by referring to a law dictionary to try to understand the terms used. Early efforts will be more productive if you have a basic understanding of civil procedure terms and the fundamental aspects of case analysis, and then follow the strategies for reading cases that are outlined at the end of this chapter.

A. Basic Civil Procedure[3]

The person who believes he was harmed begins civil litigation by filing a *complaint* in the court he selects. The *plaintiff* is the person who files the complaint; the person against whom the complaint is filed is the *defendant*. The complaint names the parties, states the facts, notes the relevant laws, and asks for relief. Courts vary considerably in how much information is required at this stage of the litigation. In Idaho, the complaint must be specific enough to put the defendant on notice of the legal concerns at issue and to allow her to prepare a defense.

The defendant has a limited amount of time in which to file a response to this complaint. One form of response to the complaint is an *answer*. In the answer, the defendant admits to the parts of the complaint that she knows are true, denies those things that she disputes, and asserts no knowledge of other allegations. The defendant also may raise affirmative defenses. (If the defendant does nothing within the prescribed time, the plaintiff can ask the court for a *default judgment*, which would grant the plaintiff the relief sought in the complaint.)

Throughout the litigation, parties submit a variety of papers to the court for its consideration. Some require no action or response from the court, for example, the filing of the complaint. In other instances, a party asks the court to make a decision or take action. An example is a motion for summary judgment, where a party asks the court to decide in that party's favor without the need for a trial.

When the trial judge grants a motion that ends a case, the losing party can appeal. The appealing party is called the *appellant*; the other party is the *respondent*.[4] In deciding an appeal from an order granting a motion, the appellate court is deciding whether the trial judge was correct in issuing the order at that stage of the litigation. If the appellate court agrees with the decision of the trial judge, it will *affirm*. If not, the court will *reverse* the order granting the motion and, in some instances, *remand* the case back to the trial court.

---

3. A parallel process works in criminal cases. See the local rules of criminal procedure for details.

4. In most jurisdictions, the terms appellant-appellee are used when a party has a right to appeal, while the terms petitioner-respondent apply to parties when the court has discretion to hear the appeal. Idaho uses the term respondent for the non-moving party in both instances.

Even at trial, the parties might make motions that can be appealed. For example, during the trial, the plaintiff presents his evidence first. After all of the plaintiff's witnesses have testified, the defendant may move for a *judgment as a matter of law*, arguing that the plaintiff cannot win based on the evidence presented and asking for an immediate decision. An order granting that motion could be appealed.

Most of the reported cases are appeals of orders granting motions. These cases apply different standards of review, depending on the motion that is the object of the appeal. While standards of review are beyond the scope of this book, understanding the procedural posture of the case is crucial to understanding the court's holding. The relevant rules of civil procedure will guide your analysis.

B. Analyzing the Substance of Cases

Novice researchers often find it difficult to determine whether a case is relevant to a particular research problem and if so how to use the case. This section explains how to analyze cases to determine their relevance.

If the case concerns the same legally significant facts as your client's situation and the court applies law on point for your problem, then the case is relevant. Legally significant facts are those that affect the court's decision. Some attorneys call these outcome-determinative facts, key facts, or material facts. The facts that are legally significant depend on the case. The height of the defendant in a contract dispute is unlikely to be legally significant, but that fact may be critical in a criminal case where the only eyewitness testified that the thief was about five feet tall.

Rarely will your research reveal a case with facts that are exactly the same as your client's situation. Rather, several cases may involve facts that are similar to your client's situation but not exactly the same. Your job is to determine whether the facts are similar enough for a court to apply the law in the same way and reach the same outcome. If the court reached a decision favorable to your client, you will highlight the similarities. If, on the other hand, the court reached an unfavorable decision from your client's perspective, you may argue that the case is distinguishable from yours based on its facts or that its reasoning is faulty. You have an ethical duty to ensure that the court knows about a case directly on point, even if the outcome of that case is adverse to your client.

You are also unlikely to find one case that addresses all aspects of your client's situation. Most legal claims have several elements or factors. *Elements* are required subparts of a claim, while *factors* are important aspects but not required. If a court decides that one element is not met, it may not discuss others. In a different case, the court may decide that two factors are so overwhelming that others have no impact on the outcome. In these circumstances, you would have to find additional cases that analyze the other elements or factors.

Even if a case is relevant to some portion of your analysis, you still must decide how heavily to weigh it in your analysis. Two important points need to be considered here. One is the concept of *stare decisis*; the other is the difference between the holding of the case and dicta within that case.

Stare decisis means "to stand by things decided."[5] This means that courts must follow prior judicial opinions, ensuring consistency in the application of the law. This requirement, however, is limited to the courts within one jurisdiction. The Idaho Court of Appeals must follow the decisions of the Idaho Supreme Court, but not those of the courts of any other state. The concept of *stare decisis* also refers to a court with respect to its own opinions. The Court of Appeals, thus, should follow its own earlier cases in deciding new matters. If a court decides not to continue following its earlier cases, it is usually because of changes in society that have outdated the law of the earlier case, or because a new statute has been enacted that changes the legal landscape.

Under *stare decisis*, courts are required to follow the holdings of prior cases. A *holding* is the court's ultimate decision on the matter of law at issue in the case. The holding is the court's determination of whether a legal standard has been met. This is different from the procedural dispositions, such as affirming or remanding.

Other statements or observations included in the opinion are not binding; they are referred to as *dicta*. For example, a court in a contract dispute may hold that the defendant breached the contract. In reaching that decision, the court may note that had the facts been slightly different, it would have decided that no breach occurred. That observation is not binding on future courts, though it may be cited as persuasive authority.

After finding a number of cases that have similar facts, that discuss the same legal issue, and that are binding on your client, the next step is to synthesize the cases to state and explain the legal rule. Sometimes a court states the rule fully; if not, piece together the information from the relevant cases to state the rule completely but concisely. Then use the analysis and facts of various

---

5. *Black's Law Dictionary* 1443 (Bryan A. Garner ed., 8th ed., West 2004).

cases to explain the law. Decide how the rule applies to the client's facts, and determine your conclusion. Note that this method of synthesis is much more than mere summaries of all the various cases.

C. Strategies for Reading Cases

As you begin reading cases, the following strategies may help you understand them more quickly and more thoroughly.

- Review the background and holdings quickly to determine whether the case seems to be on point. If so, skim the headnotes to find the particular portion of the case that is relevant. Remember that one case may discuss several issues of law, only one or two of which may interest you. Go to the portion of the case identified by the relevant headnote and decide whether it is important for your project.
- If so, skim the entire case to get a feeling for what happened and why, focusing on the portion of the case identified by the relevant headnote.
- Next, read the case slowly and carefully. Skip the parts that are obviously not pertinent to your problem. For example, if you are researching a contract question, there is no need to scrutinize a tort issue that is not pertinent to your contract question.
- At the end of each paragraph or page, consider what you have read. If you cannot summarize it, try reading the material again.
- The next time you read the case, take notes. The notes may be in the form of a formal "case brief" or they may be scribbles that only you can understand. Regardless of the form, the process of taking notes will help you parse through, identify, and comprehend the essential concepts of the case.
- Note that skimming text online or highlighting a printed page is often not sufficient to achieve thorough comprehension of judicial opinions.

Often you will read groups of cases as you conduct research. Reading the cases and understanding the law will be easier if you organize your approach. First, organize groups of cases according to jurisdiction and then by decision date. Learning how the law developed over time in each jurisdiction will be easier if you read the cases chronologically. Alternatively, finding the current rule of law will likely be easier if you begin with the most recent cases. Define your goal and organize the order in which you read the cases accordingly.

Pay attention to how the cases fit together. Look for trends in the law and in the facts of the cases. Has the law remained unchanged or have new elements been introduced? Has the meaning of an important term been redefined? Have certain facts virtually guaranteed success for one party while other facts have tended to cause difficulties? Does one case summarize the current rule, or do you have to synthesize a rule from several cases that each address part of the rule? Answers to these fundamental questions should guide your analysis of the judicial opinions.

Chapter 12

Citators

Courts expect lawyers to update every authority on which they rely to ensure that the attorneys' arguments are well supported by current law.[1] Attorneys do this using *citators*. Citators are tools that list all subsequent sources that have cited to a particular legal authority. However, beyond ensuring that arguments are supported by current law, citators provide a powerful research tool. Citators not only allow you to determine if an authority is still good law, they allow you to expand your research results because they provide connections to other authorities that may also be relevant to your client's problem.

Although Chapter 1 lists updating as the fifth step in the legal research process, you should use a citator at several different points in your research process. First, a glance at a citator's overall assessment of an authority allows you to determine quickly whether you will need to determine the subsequent treatment of that authority before relying on it to solve your client's problem. Second, once you have read a case thoroughly and decided that it is important for answering the client's question, you can update it carefully noting both cases that expand on the legal issue and any cases that criticize or distinguish the case. Those cases could be used against your client.

Third, use the list of results a citator provides to expand your research results. Carefully reviewing the list could reveal other cases or secondary sources that discuss the same point of law, and these authorities might have clearer reasoning or more facts that are more analogous to your client's. Finally, use a citator to check all the authorities in your work before you submit your final document to a partner or a court, and right before oral arguments.

Many types of legal authority can be updated with a citator: cases, statutes, constitutional provisions, regulations, and some secondary sources. This chap-

---

1. *See e.g. In re Tway*, 128 Idaho 794, 796, 919 P.2d 323, 325 (1996) (suspending attorney for neglecting client's claim after noting that he "had not Shepardized the cases he relied on regarding the statute of limitations").

ter, however, will use a case to explain the process of updating. For other sources, you should follow the same process.

I. Citator Fundamentals

Online citators provide the most efficient way to update authorities and expand research. The two most well-known online services provide the most robust citators. "Shepard's" is the online citator available on Lexis; Westlaw provides a comparable service called "KeyCite."[2] The legal sources included in Shepard's and KeyCite are not identical, and the two services are always expanding. It is a good idea to check the coverage periodically. Generally, all federal primary authority can be Shepardized and KeyCited. In addition, most state statutes and cases are included in both services. The coverage of state administrative law varies.[3]

Understanding citators requires familiarity with two basic terms: the cited source and the citing sources. The authority you are updating is called the *cited source*. The authorities listed in a citator that refer to that case are called *citing sources* or *citing references*. Once you have accessed the cited source using a citator, the work of updating is aided by the context and connectivity provided by the service. While the citator provides you with a list of citing sources, the main work of updating comes from reading these citing sources and using the features of the citator to determine on your own whether the case is still good law. Table 12-1 summarizes the process for using online citators.

A. Accessing and Reading the Citator List

Using the online services to compile a list of citations is quite easy; for each service, simply type a citation in the appropriate box and run the search. Understanding the search results can be difficult and tedious at first, but it becomes easier with practice. Even so, using citators is almost always a time-consuming activity, primarily because of the number of sources that must be read and analyzed.

Shepard's is available from two points on Lexis. If you are already viewing a document, click on the "Shepardize this document" link in the right-hand

---

2. These online citators are the focus of this chapter, though other online services provide citators and *Shepard's Citations* provides a print citator.
3. Be aware that an authority may be included in one of the services only for purposes of expanding research, not for determining whether the authority is still valid.

Table 12-1. Outline for Using Online Citators

1. Access the citator and enter the citation of the cited source in the box provided.
2. Review the analytical symbols provided by the citator.
3. Select the type of citation list needed: a short list showing the direct history and negative treatment of the cited source, or a longer list showing all subsequent citing references.
4. Limit the list of citing references by jurisdiction, headnote, date, or other function.
5. Prioritize and read the citing references. Analyze the impact, if any, these sources have on the authority being updating.

menu. Otherwise, enter "shep:" in the search box, followed by the citation of the cited source. The KeyCite system can be accessed two ways: (1) by typing "keycite" or "kc" prior to any citation in the search box on the home page, and (2) from any document on Westlaw by using the "Negative Treatment," "History," and "Citing Reference" tabs. The KeyCite link leads to a pop-up screen that includes an overview of analysis symbols used.

To determine whether a citing source might affect whether the case is still good law, you can simply click on the citing source and go to the point in that source that discussed the cited source. Quickly reading that portion of the source will reveal whether that source is relevant to your research. Some citing sources will not address the legal issue you are researching. If the citing source does address that legal issue, you should read it more carefully to analyze the impact on the problem you are solving. Did the citing source change the meaning of the law? Did it apply the law to a new fact pattern? Did it distinguish the citied source? And if so, how and why?

B. Review Analytical Symbols

Both Shepard's and KeyCite provide colored symbols to give researchers a basic understanding of the validity of the cited source. Red symbols suggest negative treatment (perhaps the case has been overruled), while blue and green symbols suggest neutral or positive treatment by later sources. Do not give these symbols more weight than they deserve.[4] A red symbol may mean that

---

4. Always read and analyze the citing references carefully, especially when determining whether a source is still good law. A recent survey determined that KeyCite and Shepard's results were in error 33% and 38% of the time, respectively. Paul Hellyer,

Table 12-2. Analytical Symbols for Lexis and Westlaw

Lexis	
Red	Warns that your case has negative treatment (overruled or reversed)
Orange	Questions the continuing validity of your case
Yellow	Indicates serious negative treatment (criticized)
Green	Positive treatment
Blue	Neutral treatment
Westlaw	
Red Flag	Negative treatment; the case is no longer good law for at least one point of law.
Orange Circle	The case may no longer be good for at least one point of law based on its reliance on an overruled or otherwise invalid prior decision.
Yellow Flag	Some negative treatment, but the case hasn't been overruled or reversed.
Blue/White Flag	A federal case has an appeal pending

the case was overruled in part; if the portion of the case that affects your project was not overruled, that portion is still good law. On both services, the colored symbols simply provide a quick visual. Make sure to review the service's explanation of the significance of each symbol. Table 12-2 lists the analytical symbols for Lexis and Westlaw.

C. Select Citation List Needed and Filter Results

Citators can return long lists of citing sources and reading every one would be unreasonable and ineffective. Thus, once you have accessed the cited source, you will need to determine which citator list you need and use filters to narrow the results. Prioritize the results based on the following: 1) Read citing cases that treat your case negatively. 2) Read cases from the controlling jurisdiction. 3) Read cases from the highest appellate court in the controlling jurisdiction. 4) Read more recent cases first. 5) Read cases that deal with the same legal issues as your case.

Lexis provides four different lists within Shepard's.

Evaluating Shepard's, KeyCite, and BCite for Case Validation Accuracy, 110 Law Libr. J. 449, 465 (2018).

- Appellate History: Lists to cases in the same litigation as your case.
- Citing Decisions: Refers to all cases, except those in the same litigation, that have subsequently cited your case.
- Other Citing Sources: Lists secondary sources and court briefs that cite your case.
- Table of Authorities: Lists all of the cases cited by the case you are updating.

Once you have accessed a list on Shepard's, the resulting screen will allow you to narrow the results by selecting filters from the left-hand side of the screen or to sort the results using a dropdown menu to organize by analysis, discussion, court, or date. You can also use the symbols and "Depth of Discussion" bars next to the citing cases to prioritize which cases you should review. When reviewing the list, recognize that the symbol next to the citing case refers to that case's treatment. Look for the colored symbol under the citing case's citation and the legend to the right side of the screen for the depth of discussion bars and headnote number

Westlaw also provides four different lists from the top of any case.

- Negative Treatment: Shows any negative treatment of your case from either within the same litigator or from other litigation.
- History: Lists all the cases in the same litigation, regardless of their positive or negative treatment of your case.
- Citing References: Refers to all the citing cases in other litigation.
- Table of Authorities: Lists the cases cited by the case you are updating.

Westlaw provides several options for limiting results. To review only subsequent negative treatment, choose that tab. The resulting list will have "Depth of Treatment" bars. Also any of the citing cases that have negative treatment will have a colored symbol next to their citation in the list. Westlaw provides several additional options for filtering from the broadest list "Citing References." After selecting the "Citing References" tab, you can filter from a dropdown menu above the list; you can also organize the results by court, date, or depth of treatment. From the left-hand side of the screen you can limit your review by documents type, i.e. cases or secondary sources. Finally, you can filter the results by search term, jurisdiction, date, depth of treatment, headnote, treatment status of the citing case, and whether the citing case is reported or unreported.

D. Read the Results

Regardless of which list you use and which filters you apply, you must still read and analyze the citing cases that are relevant to your project. You must ensure that each source you rely on is still good law. Make sure to carefully evaluate any impact they might have and to determine if you may want to add that citing case to your answer.

E. Alerts

Both Lexis and Westlaw allow you to set an alert function that will monitor your cited authorities and let you know of recent action. For example, you could request a weekly email notifying you of any new negative treatment of a case crucial to your analysis. On Lexis, the you can create an alert from any Shepard's screen by clicking on the button with the bell icon at the top of the screen after the cited source's citation. On Westlaw, click the link "Notifications" at the top right of any screen, then select "Alert." The select "Create Alert" from the resulting screen.

Chapter 13

Legal Citation

I. Citation as Language

Lawyers use legal citations to demonstrate that their arguments are well researched and their analysis is well supported. While new law students are tempted at times to skip over citations in documents that they read, experienced attorneys read legal citations as easily as they read textual sentences. Essentially, legal citations tell the reader where to find the authorities relied on and indicate the level of analytical support the authorities provide.[1] Thus, while legal citations are succinct, they convey a depth of meaning to a law-trained reader.

II. Purpose of Legal Citations

Legal citation allows us to write in a form that quickly and succinctly gives the reader helpful information about the support and research that underpins a particular piece of legal writing.[2] "The difference between writing and *legal writing* is, of course, the law. To write about law, one must first do legal research. A careful legal writer then conveys to the reader the thoroughness of that research and the support of various authorities through citations."[3]

---

1. ALWD & Colleen M. Barger, *ALWD Guide to Legal Citation*, 2 (6th ed., Aspen Publishers 2017) ("*ALWD Guide*").
2. The Legal Information Institute, *Purpose of Legal Citation; Introduction to Basic Legal Citation, § 1-220*, https://www.law.cornell.edu/citation/1-200.
3. Suzanne E. Rowe, *Signaling Support: Linking Citation to Text*, https://www.osbar.org/publications/bulletin/08nov/legalwriter.html (emphasis in original).

Instead of forcing the reader to wade through extraneous chaff, correct legal citations efficiently guide the reader to the precise pin-point of referenced authority. To do so, accurate legal citations accomplish four purposes:

1. Instruct the reader on locating a source.
2. Inform the reader about the weight and persuasiveness of a source.
3. Convey the type and degree of support for a proposition.
4. Demonstrate the author's thorough research.

III. Principles of Legal Citation

Legal citation conveys information succinctly and efficiently by adhering to four principles. Thus, legal citation follows the 1) core identification principles, 2) minimum content principles, 3) compacting principles, and 4) formatting principles.[4]

A. Core Identification Principles

Each citation must contain certain, core information in order to allow the reader to retrieve the authority. If a citation lacks the necessary information, a reader will be unable to ensure the accuracy of the textual sentence. For instance, try to retrieve either of the following:

Sopatyk at 812

Community for Creative Non-Violence v. Reid, U.S. 730, 735.

Neither of these citations adheres to the principle of giving the reader the minimum information necessary to retrieve the citation. For cases, citations need to include party names; reporter information, including volume and page numbers; and court identification information. For statutes, citations need to include the code, the title, and section.

B. Minimum Content Principles

Citations need additional information beyond just that necessary to allow the reader to find the authority. While the following citation meets the core identification principle, it doesn't contain the minimum content a reader expects. *Sopatyk*, 151 Idaho 809, 812.

---

4. The Legal Information Institute, *Types of Citation Principles*, § 1-300, https://www.law.cornell.edu/citation/1-300.

For cases and statutes, citations need to include dates. For cases, other information might also be necessary, such as the deciding court or subsequent history. For articles and books, the author and edition must be identified. (For some content, the lack of inclusion shows that something doesn't exist—for instance, we don't indicate a book is the first edition until there is a second edition).

C. Compacting Principles

Remember that legal citations are meant to be short and efficient. Thus, legal citations include standardized abbreviations and eliminate redundancy.

Consider this example: 42 United States Code Section 1983 (2007). This meets both the core identification principle and the minimum content principle, but it is not compact. Instead, the compact citation would be 42 U.S.C. § 1983 (2007) because codes are abbreviated and citations use typographic symbols.

D. Formatting Principles

Finally, citations follow certain formatting principles. Legal writers use certain fonts, certain punctuation, and order the elements of a citation in a specific way. So, while you could find the following case, it's hard to read the citation because it doesn't follow the formatting principles. Tinker v. Des Moines Indep. Cmty. Sch. Dist., (1969) at 506, 393 U.S. 503.

The remainder of this chapter addresses the specific format used to convey citation information. Because much citation information is given in abbreviated form, using a uniform and widely recognized format ensures that the reader will understand the information being conveyed. In Idaho, attorneys follow general practices in citation that are familiar to the Idaho legal community; those will be explained first. Then the chapter turns to the two national citation manuals, the *ALWD: Guide to Legal Citation*[5] and *The Bluebook: A Uniform System of Citation*.[6] In other states, you may encounter state statutes, court rules, and various style manuals that dictate the form of citation used before the courts of different states. Law firms or agencies sometimes adopt their own preference for citation or make minor variations to generally accepted formats. Once you are aware of the basic function and format of citation, adapting to a slightly different set of rules is not difficult.

---

5. *Id.*
6. *The Bluebook: A Uniform System of Citation* (The Columbia Law Review et al. eds., 20th ed., The Harvard Law Review Assn. 2016) ("*Bluebook*").

IV. Idaho Citation — General Practices

Most states have their own rules of citation, called *local rules*. These rules differ somewhat from the rules of other states and the rules in the two national citation manuals. While there is no book or manual that dictates Idaho citation format, general practices have developed. Some are drawn from Idaho statutes and others are based on Idaho Supreme Court rules. Examples are shown in Table 13-1. Note that the Idaho Supreme Court has issued Internal Rule 15(e) that allows citation according to either the *ALWD Guide* or the *Bluebook* whenever no Idaho statute or Supreme Court rule applies.

Table 13-1. Example Citations Under Idaho Conventions

Constitution:	Idaho Const. art. VIII, § 3.
Statutes:	I.C. § 33-512B.
Cases:	*State v. Jeppesen*, 138 Idaho 71, 57 P.3d 782 (2002).
State Rules:	IDAPA 38.05.01.060.02.c.ii.

V. Other States' Citation Rules

When working in another state, follow that state's local rules or use the format given in the *ALWD Guide* or the *Bluebook*, depending on your office's preferences. In Oregon, for example, the appellate courts publish a style manual to be followed by documents submitted to the Oregon Supreme Court and Oregon Court of Appeals. The abbreviations required by that style manual are familiar to lawyers practicing in Oregon and are used even in documents not to be submitted to court.

VI. National Citation Manuals

The two most widely used national citation manuals are the *ALWD Guide* and the *Bluebook*. Both are large booklets that contain hundreds of pages of citation rules, examples, and explanations.

The *ALWD Guide* is considered by many the best citation manual for novices and for practitioners. The explanations are clear, and it contains examples for both the format required in the memoranda and briefs attorneys write and for academic writing within a single rule.

The *Bluebook* is the oldest, most widely known citation manual. The difficulty with this manual is that most of the *Bluebook*'s explanations and examples are relevant to law review footnotes, which use different fonts (e.g., italics, large and small capitals) than citations in practice documents. In order to create citations for practice documents, users must consult the main rule and then modify the examples using a second set of rules. Even so, the *Bluebook* is so well known that most attorneys use the term "Bluebooking" to mean checking citations for consistent format.

A. Navigating the *ALWD Guide* and the *Bluebook*

The *ALWD Guide* and the *Bluebook* are reference manuals, like dictionaries and thesauri. It is important to learn their general structure and how to use them, not to read them cover-to-cover.

1. Index

The index at the back of each manual is quite extensive, and in most instances it is more helpful than the table of contents. Most often, you should begin working with a citation manual by referring to the index.

2. "Fast Formats" and "Quick Reference"

Many chapters of the *ALWD Guide* begin with citation examples, in tables called "Fast Formats." A list of these "Fast Formats" is provided on the inside front cover of the *ALWD Guide*.

The *Bluebook* contains two "Quick Reference" guides. The one on the inside front cover provides sample citations for law review footnotes. The guide on the inside back cover gives example citations for court documents and legal memoranda.

3. *Bluebook* "Bluepages"

The *Bluebook* opens with a section devoted to citations for practitioners; these "Bluepages" appear on pages 3 through 56. The Bluepages provide information for and additional examples of citations used in documents other than law review articles.[7] When using the *Bluebook*, remember that only the

---

7. The Bluepages are helpful in knowing which font to use in practice document citations. The Bluepages list the following items that should be italicized or underlined in citations in legal memoranda and court documents: case names, titles of books and articles, and introductory signals. Items not included in the list should appear in regular

Table 13-2. Example Citations in *ALWD* and *Bluebook* Format

Type of Document	*ALWD* and *Bluebook* Format
Constitution	Idaho Const. art. VIII, § 3.
Statutes	Idaho Code Ann. § 73-201 (2006).
Cases	*State v. Jeppesen*, 138 Idaho 71, 57 P.3d 782 (2002).
State Rules	Idaho Admin. Code r. 38.05.01.060.02.c.ii (2006).

Bluepages and the reference guide at the back of the manual provide examples for practice documents. Thus, a student or lawyer using the *Bluebook* has to use the Bluepages to translate other examples from law review format into the format used in legal documents in practice.

4. *ALWD* Appendices and *Bluebook* Tables

The back of each citation manual contains lists of abbreviations and other helpful information. In the *ALWD Guide* these are called "appendices."[8] Pages with a dark blue stripe at the back of the *Bluebook* contain "tables," with similar information.[9]

B. Citing Idaho Material

Because these manuals are designed for national use, their abbreviations for some Idaho material vary from Idaho practice. A summary of abbreviations for Idaho material appears in Appendix 1 (on page 362–63) of the *ALWD Guide* and in Table T1.3 (on page 261) of the *Bluebook*. Examples are included in Table 13-1 in this section. Compare these examples to the Idaho citations shown in Table 13-2.

---

type. Remember to follow the instructions in the Bluepages even when other *Bluebook* examples include large and small capital letters.

8. *ALWD* pages 345–518. Especially helpful are Appendix 1 (federal reporters), pages 346–49; Appendix 3 (months, case names), pages 439, 444–47; Appendix 4 (courts), pages 451–58; and Appendix 5 (periodicals), pages 459–505.

9. *Bluebook* pages 233–522. Especially helpful are Table T1.1 (federal reporters), pages 233–36; Table T.6 (case names), pages 496–98; Table T.12 (months), page 510; and Table T.13 (periodicals), pages 510–17.

C. Incorporating Citations into a Document

A legal document must provide a citation for each idea that comes from a case, statute, article, or other source. Thus, paragraphs that state legal rules and explain the law should contain many citations.[10]

A citation may offer support for an entire sentence or for an idea expressed in part of a sentence. If the citation supports the entire sentence, it is placed in a separate *citation sentence* that begins with a capital letter and ends with a period.[11] If the citation supports only a portion of the sentence, it is included immediately after the relevant part of that sentence and set off from the sentence by commas in what is called a *citation clause*.[12] Table 13-3 provides examples of each.

Table 13-3. Examples of Citation Sentences and Citation Clauses*

Citation Sentences: Certain general procedures apply to the reinstatement of all suspended driver's licenses. I.C. § 49-328. Additional procedures apply if a judicial suspension became effective after release from imprisonment. I.C. § 49-326A.
Citation Clauses: In all instances of suspended driver's license reinstatement, certain general procedures apply, I.C. § 49-328, and additional procedures apply when a judicial suspension became effective after release from imprisonment, I.C. § 49-326A.

* Note that the citations in this table are in Idaho format, not the longer versions required by the national manuals.

Do not cite a client's facts or your conclusions about a case, statute, or other authority. The following sentence should not be cited: "Our client must follow only the general procedures for driver's license reinstatement." These facts and conclusions are unique to your situation and would not be found anywhere in the reference source.

---

10. *ALWD* Rule 34.2, page 298; *Bluebook* Rule B1.1, pages 3–4. Note that the rule numbers are likely to remain the same in subsequent editions of each manual, though the page numbers will probably change.
11. *ALWD* Rule 34.1(a), page 294; *Bluebook* Rule B1.1, page 3–4.
12. *ALWD* Rule 34.1(b), page 295; *Bluebook* Rule B1.1, page 3–4.

D. Case Citations
1. Full Citations to Cases

A full citation to a case includes the following elements in this order.[13] The discussion below uses the following example.

> EXAMPLE: *Flint v. Dennison*, 488 F.3d 816, 820 (9th Cir. 2007).

- *The name of the case.*

Include the name of just the first party on each side, even if several are listed in the case caption. If the party is an individual, include only the party's last name. If the party is a business or organization, shorten the party's name by using abbreviations provided in the citation manual you are using.[14]

Between the parties' names, place a lower case "v" followed by a period. Do not use a capital "V" or the abbreviation "vs." Place a comma after the second party's name, but do not italicize or underline this comma.

The parties' names may be italicized or underlined. Use the style preferred by your office and use that style consistently throughout each document.[15] Do not combine italics and underlining in one cite or within a single document.

- *The volume and reporter in which the case is published.*

Next, give the volume and the reporter in which the case is found.[16] Pay special attention to whether the reporter is in its first, second, or third series.[17] In the *Flint* example above, 488 is the volume number and F.3d is the reporter abbreviation for *Federal Reporter, Third Series.*

---

13. *ALWD* Rule 12, pages 55–100; *Bluebook* Rule B10, pages 94–118.
14. *ALWD* Appendix 3, pages 444–47; *Bluebook* Table T.6, pages 496–98.
15. *ALWD* Rule 12.2 (case names), page 59 and Rule 1.1 (typeface choice), page 10; *Bluebook* Rule B2, page 6.
16. For cases available only on Lexis or Westlaw, follow *ALWD* Rules 12.13 (forthcoming publications) page 93 or rule 12.14 (unpublished cases) page 93–95 and *Bluebook* Rule B 10.1.4, page 14–15.
17. Abbreviations for common reporters are found in chart 12.2 on page 75–76 of the *ALWD Guide*; abbreviations for reporters for Idaho cases are included on pages 362–63. The *Bluebook* does not have a comprehensive list of common reporters; check Table T.1 on pages 233–306 for reporters in a particular jurisdiction. Abbreviations for reporters for Idaho cases are given in the *Bluebook* on page 261.

- ***The first page of the case followed by the exact page in the case that contains the idea you are citing (i.e., the* pinpoint *or* jump *cite).***

After the reporter name, include both the first page of the case and the pinpoint page containing the idea that you are referencing, separated by a comma and a space.[18] The first page of the *Flint* case above is 816, and the page containing the specific idea being cited is 820. If the pinpoint page you are citing is also the first page of the case, then the same page number will appear twice.[19]

- ***The court that decided the case.***

In a parenthetical following this information, indicate the court that decided the case.[20] In Appendix 1 of the *ALWD Guide* and in Table T.1 of the *Bluebook*, the notations for the courts of each jurisdiction are included in parentheses just after the name of the court. In the *Flint* example, the Ninth Circuit Court of Appeals, a federal court, decided the case.

If the reporter abbreviation clearly indicates which court decided a case, do not repeat this information in the parenthetical. To give an example, only cases of the United States Supreme Court are reported in *United States Reports*, abbreviated U.S. Repeating court notation (U.S.) in citations to that reporter would be duplicative. By contrast, *Pacific Reporter, Third Series*, abbreviated P.3d, publishes decisions from different courts within nine states, so the court that decided a particular case needs to be indicated parenthetically. Thus, in the last example below, "Cal." indicates that the decision came from the California Supreme Court rather than from another court whose decisions are also published in this reporter.

---

18. *ALWD* Rule 5, pages 27–32 and Rule 12.5, pages 79–80; *Bluebook* Rule B10.1.2, page 12.

19. When using an online version of a case, remember that a reference to a specific reporter page may change in the middle of a computer screen or a printed page. Thus, the page number indicated at the top of the screen or printed page may not be the page where the relevant information is located. For example, if the notation *821 appeared in the text before the relevant information, the pinpoint cite would be to page 821, not page 820.

20. *ALWD* Rule 12.6(a), page 81; *Bluebook* Rule B10.1.5, page 15.

EXAMPLES: *Brown v. Bd. of Educ.*, 349 U.S. 294, 300 (1955).

State v. Perkins, 135 Idaho 17, 19 (Ct. App. 2000).

Ketchum v. Moses, 17 P.3d 735, 736 (Cal. 2001).

Note that these court abbreviations are not the same as postal codes. Abbreviating the California Supreme Court as either CA or Calif. would be incorrect. Do not use ID for the Idaho Supreme Court.

- ***The date the case was decided.***

The final piece of required information in most cites is the date the case was decided. For cases published in reporters, give only the year of decision, not the month or date.[21] Note that some cases include not only the date of decision but also the date on which the case was argued or submitted, the date on which a motion for rehearing was denied, or the publication date of the reporter. For citation, use only the year the case was decided.[22]

- ***Other parenthetical information.***

Sometimes a citation needs to show what happened to a case at an earlier or later stage of litigation. The case you are citing may have reversed an earlier case, as in the example below.

EXAMPLE: The only time that the Supreme Court addressed the requirement of motive for an EMTALA claim, the court rejected that requirement. *Roberts v. Galen of Va.*, 525 U.S. 249, 253 (1999), *rev'g* 111 F.3d 405 (6th Cir. 1997).

If you are citing a case for a court's analysis of one issue and a later court reversed only on the second issue, you need to alert your reader to that reversal. Or, if you decide for historical purposes to include in a document discussion of a case that was later overruled, your reader needs to know that as soon as you introduce the case. Prior and subsequent history can be appended to the full citations discussed above.[23]

---

21. For cases available only online, follow *ALWD* Rules 12.13 (forthcoming publications) page 93 or rule 12.14 (unpublished cases) page 93–95 and *Bluebook* Rule B 10.1.3, page 14–15.
22. *ALWD* Rule 12.7, page 83; *Bluebook* Rule B10.1.3, page 13.
23. *ALWD* Rules 12.8–12.10, pages 46–50; *Bluebook* Rule B10.2, pages 16–17.

2. Short Citations to Cases

After a full citation has been used once to introduce an authority, short citations are subsequently used to cite to the same authority. A short citation provides just enough information to allow the reader to locate the longer citation and find the pinpoint page.[24]

When the immediately preceding cite is to the same source and the same page, use *id.* as the short cite. When the second cite is to a different page within the same source, follow the *id.* with "at" and the new pinpoint page number. Capitalize *id.* when it begins a citation sentence, just as the beginning of any sentence is capitalized.[25]

If the cite is from a source that is not the immediately preceding cite, give the name of one of the parties (generally the first party named in the full cite), the volume, the reporter, and the pinpoint page following "at."[26]

> EXAMPLE: The purpose of Idaho's expert witness rules is to promote fairness and candor. *Radmer v. Ford Motor Co.*, 120 Idaho 86, 89, 813 P.2d 897, 900 (1991). The purposes of Idaho's discovery rules is to prevent surprise at trial. *Pierce v. Ollie*, 121 Idaho 539, 552, 826 P.2d 888, 901 (1992). The Idaho Supreme Court recognizes that effective cross-examination and rebuttal of expert witnesses requires advanced preparation and knowledge of that expert's testimony. *Radmer*, 120 Idaho at 89, 813 P.2d at 900.

If you refer to the case by name in the sentence, your short citation does not need to repeat the case name, though lawyers often do.[27] The last sentence of the example would also be correct as follows: "*Radmer* also recognizes that effective cross-examination and rebuttal of expert witnesses requires advanced preparation and knowledge of that expert's testimony. 120 Idaho at 89, 813 P.2d at 900."

---

24. *ALWD* Rules 11.2 and 11.3, pages 48–52; *Bluebook* Rule B4.2, pages 13–15.
25. *ALWD* Rule 11.3(d), page 49; *Bluebook* Rule B10.2, page 15.
26. *ALWD* Rule 11.2, pages 46–47 and Rule 12.16, pages 97–99; *Bluebook* Rule B10.2, page 16.
27. *ALWD* Rule 12.16(c), page 98; *Bluebook* Rule B10.2, page 16.

The format "*Radmer* at 89" consisting of just a case name and page number, is incorrect. The volume and reporter abbreviation are also needed.

E. Federal Statutory Citations

The general rule for citing federal laws is to cite the *United States Code* (U.S.C.), which is the official code for federal statutes.[28] In reality, that publication is published so slowly that the current language will most likely be found in a commercial code, either *United States Code Annotated* (published by West) or *United States Code Service* (currently published by LexisNexis).

A cite to a federal statute includes the title number, code abbreviation, section number, publisher (except for U.S.C.), and date. The date given in statutory cites is the date of the volume in which the statute is published, not the date the statute was enacted. If the language appears only in the pocket part, include only the date of the pocket part.[29] If the language of a portion of the statute is reprinted in the pocket part, include the dates of both the bound volume and the pocket part.[30]

EXAMPLE: 14 U.S.C.A. § 736 (West Supp. 2007).

(Statutory language appears in just the supplemental pocket part)

EXAMPLE: 14 U.S.C.A. § 740 (West 1990 & Supp. 2007).

(Statutory language appears in both the bound volume and the supplemental pocket part)

---

28. *ALWD* Rule 14.1, page 108; *Bluebook* Rule 12.1.1, pages 18–19 and 12.3, page 123.
29. *ALWD* Rule 8.1, page 40; *Bluebook* Rule 3.1(c), page 66.
30. *ALWD* Rule 14.2(f)(2), page 114; *Bluebook* Rule 3.1(c), page 66.

F. Signals

A citation must show the level of support each authority provides. Introductory signals show this support. The more common signals are explained below.[31]

No signal	• The source cited provides direct support for the idea in the sentence.
	• The citation identifies the source of a quotation.
See	• The source cited offers implicit support for the idea in the sentence.
	• The source cited offers support in dicta.
See also	• The source cited provides additional support for the idea in the sentence.
	• The support offered by *see also* is not as strong or direct as authorities preceded by no signal or by the signal *see*.
E.g.,	• Many authorities state the idea in the sentence, and you are citing only one as an example; this signal allows you to cite just one source while letting the reader know that many other sources say the same thing.

G. Explanatory Parentheticals

An explanatory parenthetical following a citation can convey helpful, additional information in a compressed space.[32] Sometimes this parenthetical information conveys to the reader the weight of the authority. For example, a case may have been decided *en banc* or *per curiam*. Or the case may have been decided by a narrow split among the judges who heard the case.[33] Parenthetical information also allows you to name the judges who joined in a dissenting, concurring, or plurality opinion.[34] When using this type of parenthetical, be sure that you do not inadvertently hide a critical part of the court's analysis at the end of a long citation, where a reader is likely to skip over it.

---

31. *ALWD* Rule 35, pages 300–06; *Bluebook* Rule B1.2, pages 4–5.
32. *ALWD* Rule 37, pages 314–18; *Bluebook* Rule B1.3, pages 5–6.
33. *ALWD* Rule 12.10(a), page 89; *Bluebook* Rule B10.1.5, page 15.
34. *ALWD* Rule 12.10(a), pages 89; *Bluebook* Rule B10.1.5, page 15.

EXAMPLE: Excluding relevant evidence during a sentencing hearing may deny the criminal defendant due process. *Green v. Georgia*, 442 U.S. 95, 97 (1979) (per curiam) (regarding testimony of co-defendant's confession in rape and murder case).

H. Quotations

Quotations should be used only when the reader needs to see the text exactly as it appears in the original authority. For example, quoting the controlling statutory language can be extremely helpful. As another example, if a well-known case explains an analytical point in a particularly insightful way, a quotation may be warranted.

Excessive quotation has two drawbacks. First, quotations interrupt the flow of your writing when the style of the quoted language differs from your own. Second, excessive use of quotations may suggest to the reader that you do not fully comprehend the material; it is much easier to cut and paste together a document from pieces of various cases than to synthesize and explain a rule of law. Quotations should not be used simply because you cannot think of another way to express an idea.

When a quotation is needed, the words, punctuation, and capitalization within the quotation marks must appear *exactly* as they are in the original.[35] Treat a quotation as a photocopy of the original text. Any alterations or omissions must be indicated. Include commas and periods inside quotation marks; place other punctuation outside the quotation marks unless it is included in the original text. Also, try to provide smooth transitions between your text and the quoted text.

VII. Additional Citation Details

The following citation details are second nature to careful and conscientious lawyers, though they frequently trip up novices.

- Use proper ordinal abbreviations. The most confusing are 2d for "Second" and 3d for "Third" because they differ from the standard format.[36]

---

35. *ALWD* Rules 38, 39, and 40, pages 320–41; *Bluebook*, Rule B5, pages 82–86.
36. *ALWD* Rule 4.3(b), page 26; *Bluebook* Rule 6.2(b), page 89.

- Do not insert a space between abbreviations of single capital letters. For example, there is no space in U.S. Ordinal numbers like 1st, 2d, and 3d are considered single capital letters for purposes of this rule. Thus, there is no space in P.2d or F.3d because 2d and 3d are considered single capital letters. Leave one space between elements of an abbreviation that are not single capital letters. For example, F. Supp. 2d has a space on each side of "Supp."[37]

- In citation sentences, abbreviate case names, court names, months, and reporter names. Do not abbreviate these words when they are part of textual sentences; instead, spell them out as in the example below.[38]

EXAMPLE: The Ninth Circuit held that Oregon's Measure 11 did not violate constitutional rights provided under the Eighth and Fourteenth Amendments. *Alvarado v. Hill*, 252 F.3d 1066, 1069–70 (9th Cir. 2001).

- It is most common in legal documents to spell out numbers zero through ninety-nine and to use numerals for larger numbers. However, always spell out a number that is the first word of a sentence.[39]

VIII. Citations Not Covered by a Manual

As comprehensive as the *ALWD Guide* and the *Bluebook* are, they do not definitively answer every citation question. If you cannot find a specific rule to cover a source you need to cite, look for rules regarding analogous sources. In creating a citation, always be guided by the purpose of citation: to allow a reader to find a source and to understand the type and weight of support it provides.

---

37. *ALWD* Rule 2.2, pages 15–16, *Bluebook* Rule 6.1, pages 87–88.
38. *ALWD* Rules 2.1 and 2.3, pages 15–17; *Bluebook* Rule 10.2, pages 96–102. Words like "Inc." can be abbreviated in case names in textual sentences under both manuals.
39. *ALWD* Rule 4.2(a), page 24; *Bluebook* Rule 6.2(a), page 88–89.

About the Author

Tenielle Fordyce-Ruff is an Associate Professor of Law at Concordia University School of Law, where she directs the Legal Research and Writing Program. After graduating from the University of Oregon School of Law, she clerked for Judge Joel D. Horton of the Fourth Judicial District in Idaho and then Justice Roger Burdick of the Idaho Supreme Court. She also taught legal research and writing, advanced legal research, and intensive legal writing at the University of Oregon School of Law, and was a partner in two boutique law firms in Boise.

Index

ABA Journal, 44
Administrative agencies, 4, 16, 35
Administrative enabling statute, 100
Administrative law, 97-109, 8, 10, 19, 35
Administrative Procedures Act, 98-99
Administrative regulations, 48, 100-101, 105, 107
Administrative rules, 4, 6, 8, 14, 16, 19, 94, 98-105
Advance Legislative Service, 82
Advance sheets, digests, 120-121
Advocate, The, 44, 84, 96
Agency decisions, 104-105, 108
A.L.R., *see American Law Reports*
ALWD citation,
    Cases, 146-149
    Citation clause, 145
    Citation sentence, 145, 149, 153
    Courts, 147-148
    Fast Formats, 143
    Id., 149
    Parentheticals, 148, 151-152
    Quotations, 152
    Reporters, 146, 148
    Short citation, 149
    Signals, 151
    Statutes, 150
    Typeface, 146
Amendments, constitutional, 57-58
American Jurisprudence, 41, 48
American Law Reports (A.L.R.), 36, 42, 45-46
Analytical notes, 11, 18-19
Annotations, A.L.R., 45
Annotations, constitution, 57
Annotations, statutes, 63, 68-69, 71
Appellate courts, federal, 71, 113, 122
Appellate courts, Idaho, 76, 112
Articles, *see* Legal periodicals
Articles, updating, 43
Association of Legal Writing Directors, 43, 114
Atlantic Reporter, 115-116
Attorney General opinions, 85-86

Background and holdings, 118, 130
Bankruptcy Reporter, 111
Bar journals, 44
Bill tracking, federal, 73, 87-88
Bill tracking, Idaho, 75-76
Bills, federal, 87
Bills, Idaho, 75-76

INDEX

Binding authority, 5, 119, 129
Black's Law Dictionary, 6, 129
Bluebook citation,
    Bluepages, 143-144
    Cases, 146-150
    Citation clause, 145
    Citation sentence, 145
    Courts, 147-148
    Id., 149
    Parentheticals, 148, 151-152
    Quick Reference, 143
    Quotations, 152
    Reporters, 146, 148
    Short citation, 149
    Signals, 151
    Statutes, 150
    Typeface, 146
Boolean connectors, 29-31, 125

Canons of construction, 70
Case analysis, 126-131
Case citation, 146-153, 111, 120, 123
Case digests, 23, 125-126
Case headnotes, 119-120, 125-126, 130, 137
Case reporters, 8, 68, 111, 114-121
Case research, 8, 67-69, 100
Case updating, 15, 133-137
Case verification, 133-138
Casemaker, 17, 25-26, 54, 63-64, 71, 93, 102
Certificates of review, 85
C.F.R., *see Code of Federal Regulations*
Citation form, *see ALWD* citation, *Bluebook* citation

Citators,
    Generally, 133-134
    KeyCite, 134-136
    Shepard's, 134-138
C.J.S., *see Corpus Juris Secundum*
CLE, *see* Continuing Legal Education
Code of Federal Regulations (C.F.R.), 105-107
Codified statutes,
    Federal, 71
    Idaho, 61-65
Committee minutes, legislative, 58, 74, 78-79, 83, 88, 89-90
Committee reports, legislative, 82, 87-88
Compiled legislative history, 88
Concordia University Law Review, 43
Concurring opinion, 119
Congressional Information Service (C.I.S.), 88
Constitutional interpretation, 54-56
Congressional Record, 87-89
Constitutional law research, federal, 59
Constitutional law research, Idaho, 54-56
Continuing legal education (CLE), 46
Cornell Legal Information Institute, 24-25, 71
Corpus Juris Secundum (C.J.S.), 41-42
Court rules, 93-95
CREAC, 21-22
Cumulative supplementary pamphlets, 44-45

INDEX

Current Law Index (CLI), 44-45

Daily Data, 74, 78, 83, 92
Decisions of the Federal Labor Relations Authority (F.L.R.A.), 108
DeskBook, Idaho State Bar Directory, 95-96
Deskbooks, 93
Dicta, 129, 151
Dictionary, 13, 126
Digests, 7, 23, 42, 125
Disposition, 114, 129
Dissenting opinions, 119-120, 151
District courts, 47-48, 94-95, 105, 112-113, 120-123
Docket number, 114, 118

Effect of Adoption, 58
Enabling statutes, 97-98
Enacted law, 8-9, 24
Encyclopedias, 5, 7, 35-37, 41-42
Ethics, 93-96
Executive orders, 103, 106
Explanatory parentheticals, 151

Federal administrative law, 97-98
Federal Appendix, 122
Federal cases, 121-122
Federal constitution, 59
Federal court rules, 93-95
Federal court system, 111, 113-114
Federal digests, 125
Federal judiciary, 114
Federal legislative history, 87-89
Federal Practice and Procedure, 40
Federal Practice Digest, 94-95
Federal Register, 107-108

Federal Reporter, 121-122, 146
Federal reporters, 144
Federal research,
    Administrative law, 105-109
    Cases, 121-122
    Constitutional, 59
    Digests, 125
    Legislative history, 87-89
    Reporters, 144
    Statutes, 71-72
Federal Rules Decisions, 111
Federal Rules of Evidence Service, 94-95
Federal Rules Service, 94-95
Federal statutes, 71-72
Federal Supplement, 121-122
Final Weekly Bill Status, 74, 83
FindLaw, 25, 71
Fiscal note, 58, 74, 76-78, 83
Forms, 46-48, 89, 96

Generating research terms, 13-14
Government Publishing Office, 87, 88, 89, 105, 107
Governor's Statement, 74-75
Guidance documents, 100, 104

Headnotes,
    Digests, 119, 125
    KeyCite, 135
    Reporters, 119
    Shepard's, 137
    Topic and Key Number Searching, 120
Hearings,
    Administrative, 98-99, 107-108
    Legislative, 79, 88
HeinOnline, 45, 89, 107-108

INDEX

Historical citations, legislative, 79-80, 82, 148
Hornbook, 39-41
House Journal, 78-79, 84

Idaho Administrative Bulletin, 99-100, 103
Idaho Administrative Code (IDAPA), 99, 100-102, 105, 142
Idaho Administrative Procedures Act (Idaho APA), 98-99
Idaho Administrative Rule (IDAPA), 99-100, 105
Idaho Attorney General, 73
Idaho Attorney General's Opinions and Annual Report, 85-86
Idaho Blue Book, 75, 104
Idaho case law, 13, 67-69, 100
Idaho case law, citation, 142, 146
Idaho case updating, *see* KeyCite, Shepard's
Idaho Code,
    Citation, 144
    Interpretation, 69
    Online research, 63-65
    Print research, 65-66
    Prior codifications, 82
Idaho Code (I.C.),
    Citation, 142
    Constitutional law research, 54, 56-58, 62
    Court rules research, 93-94
    Forms research, 46-48
    Legislative history research, 79-81
    Statutory research, 63-66
Idaho Code Annotated, online, 63-64

Idaho committee reports, legislative, 84-86
Idaho Constitution, 9, 53-59
Idaho Constitutional Convention, 55-56
Idaho courts, 48, 55-56, 105, 112, 116-117
Idaho Court of Appeals, 112, 114, 116-117, 120, 129
Idaho Court of Appeals Report (ICAR), 120-121
Idaho Court Rules, 93-95
Idaho Court Rules, State and Federal, 93
Idaho court system, 112
Idaho Digest, 29
Idaho district courts, 47, 104-105, 113
Idaho forms, 46-48
Idaho judiciary, 25, 39, 112, 120-121
Idaho Law Review, 43, 84
Idaho legislative history, 76-84, 89-93
Idaho Legislature, 5, 25, 27-28, 75-76
Idaho practice guides, 40-41
Idaho reporters, 114
Idaho Reports, 111, 114-121
Idaho research process, 6
Idaho Rules of Professional Conduct, 94-96
Idaho Session Laws, 66, 75, 79-82, 87
Idaho State Bar Desk Book Directory, 95-96
Idaho Supreme Court, 27, 52, 93, 95-96, 105, 112, 116, 120, 129, 142

INDEX

Idaho Supreme Court Report (ISCR), 121
Index to Legal Periodicals and Books (ILPB), 44-45
Informal Guidelines, 86
Initiative and referendum, 73, 84-86
Internet research, 3-4

Judicial decisions, 68, 100
Judicial opinions,
    Concurring, 119, 151
    Dissenting, 119, 151
    Majority, 119
    Plurality, 119, 151
Jump cite, 147
Jury instructions, 52

KeyCite, 7, 19, 43, 100, 109, 134-135
Key Number system, 32, 42, 120, 125-126

Law reviews and journals, 42-43
Legal encyclopedias, 5, 7, 41
Legal periodicals, 42-45
Legislative history research, 70, 73, 76-77, 82-84, 85, 87-89
Legislative Perspective, 78
Legislative process, 73-79, 84
LexisNexis, 17-18, 21, 25-30, 32, 38, 40-41, 43-46, 49-50, 54, 56-57, 59, 63-64, 68, 71-72, 79, 80-82, 86, 89, 93-94, 101, 103, 107-109, 122, 124-125, 134, 136, 138, 150
Library of Congress, 87, 88
Loislaw, 25
Loose-leaf services, 48-49

Majority opinion, 119
Mandatory authority, 4-7, 13, 23
Mini-library, 48
Model codes, 51-52
Monthly Matters, 78

Natural-language searching, 38-39
Ninth Circuit Court of Appeals, 147
North Eastern Reporter, 115, 116
North Western Reporter, 115, 116
Notes of decisions, 68-69
Nutshells, 39-41

Office of the Attorney General, 85-86
Online research, 4, 20-25
Online updating, 133-138
Opinions
    Attorney General opinions, 85-86
    Judicial opinions, 109-121
    Researching judicial opinions, 123-132
    Updating, 126-130

Pacific Reporter, 119, 147
Parallel citations, 116-117
Parties and procedural designations, 118
Per curiam, 119, 151
Periodicals, 36, 42-45
Persuasive authority, 5, 9, 36, 51, 85, 88, 94, 119, 129
Pinpoint page, 19, 45, 147, 149
Pocket parts,
    Annotated statutes, 66, 69, 150
    Digests, 42
Practice guides, 7, 39-41
Practicing Law Institute, 41, 46

Primary authority, 5-6, 8, 21, 23-24, 31, 35-36, 38-39, 41-42, 51, 93, 97, 99, 134
Procedural history, 58, 74, 76-78, 83
Proceedings and Debates of the Constitutional Convention of Idaho, 1889, 57
Public hearings, administrative, 98
Public law number, 87

Quoting authority, 152

Referendum, 84-86
Regional reporters, 115-116
Regulations, 5, 19, 23, 26, 48-50, 61, 100-101, 105, 107-109, 133
Reporters,
　Advance sheets, 120-121
　Case headnotes, 119
　Citation, 120-122
　Docket number, 118
　Federal cases, 121-122
　Idaho cases, 112-121
　Idaho research process, 6, 123-126
　Opinions, 109-110
Research notes, 18
Research process outlines,
　Administrative law, 100
　Bill tracking, 75
　Cases, 124
　Citators, 135
　Idaho statutes, 63
Research terms, 7-9, 11, 12-15, 17-18, 29, 33, 35, 42, 49
Research vocabulary, *see* Generating research terms
Restatements, 50-51
Rulemaking, 98, 103

Rules,
　Administrative, 98-99, 100-105
　Court, 93-96
　Ethics, 93-96
Rules of Professional Conduct, 95-96

Secondary authority, 5, 24-25, 36-38, 51
Secondary authority, updating, 134
Secondary sources,
　American Jurisprudence, 2d, 41
　American Law Reports, 45
　Articles, 35-37, 42-45
　Bar journals, 43
　Continuing legal education, 46
　Corpus Juris Secundum, 41
　Encyclopedias, 41-42
　Forms, 46-47
　Generally, 35-38
　Jury instructions, 52
　Loose-leaf services, 48-49
　Mini-libraries, 48
　Periodicals, 42-45
　Persuasive authority, 119, 129
　Practice guides, 7, 39-41
　Research process in, 35-37
　Restatements, 50-51
　Topical mini-libraries, 48-49
　Treatises, 39-40
　Uniform laws and model codes, 51-52
　Updating, generally, 49
　Use in research process, 35-37, 119, 129
Senate Journal, 78-79, 84
Session laws, 84, 87
Shepard's, 7, 43, 109, 134-135, 138
Signals, citation, 143, 151

INDEX

Slip opinions, 120, 122
Source notes, 77, 79-80
South Eastern Reporter, 115-116
South Western Reporter, 115-116
Southern Reporter, 115-116
Stare decisis, 129
State Constitutional Conventions, 8, 57
Statement of purpose, 58, 74, 76-78, 83, 91
Statement of Meaning and Purpose, 58
Statutes,
    Canons of construction, 70
    Citation, 63, 65, 142, 144, 150
    Definitions, 20, 66
    Enabling, 97
    Idaho research, 63-71
    Online, 63-65
    Pocket parts, 66, 69, 150
    Research process, 63-71
    Updating, 135, 137
Statutes at Large, 87
Statutory construction, 70
Statutory research, federal, 71
Statutory research, Idaho, 61-69
Supreme Court of the United States, 113
Supreme Court Reporter (S. Ct.), 121-122
Supreme Court Reporter, Lawyers' Edition (L. Ed. 2d), 121
Synopsis, 32, 118

Table-of-contents searching, 27-28, 63
TARPP, 13-14
Term of art, 14
Term of court, 118

Terms-and-connectors searching, 28-31, 38, 64, 125
Topic searching, 28, 32, 125
Topical mini-library, 48-49
Topical reporters, 111
Treatises, 5, 7, 16, 36, 39-41
Trial courts, 111-114, 122, 127

Uniform laws, 51-52
Uniform Laws Annotated, 52
United States Code (U.S.C.), 71, 105, 150
United States Code Annotated (U.S.C.A.), 71
United States Code Congressional and Administrative News (U.S.C.C.A.N.), 88
United States Code Service (U.S.C.S.), 71
United States Constitution, 113, 54, 59
United States Courts of Appeals, 113
United States District Courts, 122-123
United States Law Week, 122
United States Reports (U.S.), 122
United States Statutes at Large, 122, 147
United States Supreme Court, 122, 147, 113
Unofficial reporters, 115
Unpublished opinions, 114, 122
Unreported opinions, 114, 122,
Updating,
    Federal regulations, 108
    Generally, 134
    Idaho administrative rules, 103, 108

Lexis, 135
Process, 134-137
Westlaw, 135

VersusLaw, 25-26
Veto, 74-75

Westlaw, 17-18, 20-21, 25-28, 30, 32, 40-41, 43-46, 49-50, 54, 56-57, 59, 63-65, 71, 89, 93-94, 100-101, 103, 107-109, 117, 119, 123-126, 134-138
West's Idaho Code Annotated (W.I.C.A.), 63, 65
Words and Phrases, 120